Oregon Bill's

Heart
and Soul

Moms —
Stories from a sage +
dear curmudgeon.

Enjoy!

& April Craig

Oregon Bill's

Heart and Soul

by Rod Fielder

Flapjack Press
Brownsville, OR
2010

The author would like to thank the
Brownsville Times Newspaper where
these essays originally appeared.

The author would also like to thank
Rick Coxen for the photographs
appearing in the book.

Front Cover:

Three Totems

Material: cast bronze, walnut stump, green serpentine stone
60" height, 5" width, 22" depth
Owner: Artist

Back Cover:

Leggy

Material: wood and brick
22" height, 6" width, 4" depth
Owner: Artist

ISBN 978-1-4507-1787-8

Flapjack Press, 36176 Hwy. 228
Brownsville, Oregon 97327
541-466-5589

Printed by Gorham Printing, WA

For our children:

Kristina Hollerman   **Steve Miller**
Kathryn Fielder   **Ann Francis Miller**
Rick Fielder   **Nancy Miller Haas**
Pieter Fielder

From my heart

Phillipi I

Material: found cast iron and stone, 60" height, 5" width, 24" depth

Owners: Dick and Marie Keis, Corvallis, Oregon

Oregon Bill's
Heart and Soul

Cardiac Thrills

Busting Out of Prison

On The Path

Cardiac Thrills

Phillipi IV

Material: found cast iron and deer horn, 65" height, 5" width, 29" depth
Owner: Artist

Talk About a Thrill

There are lots of thrills this old life offers but Oregon Bill recommends a good solid heart attack as the thrill of thrills. Every fiber in your body gets electrified when you recognize what that dull pain in your chest and arm probably means.

And, time slows down. Way down. You know how it is when you are doing something really well, say hitting a fast ball against a pitcher throwing serious smoke…time gets really slow. You can count the silent ticks inside a minute. Hell, you can count the ticks inside a second. That's what the thrill of a coronary is like.

But even a coronary is worth a giggle and a snicker if you go at it right. Here are a couple of laughs on Oregon Bill. First, the giggle.

Long time after my heart attack, when I was back jogging everyday and feeling fit, the Doc thought he detected a skipped beat when I was doing a stress test on the treadmill. Hated those tests. Wires hanging everywhere recording little spikes on paper rolling right there in front of your eyes. Then they point that treadmill toward the ceiling just like you were climbing to heaven and getting nowhere. But, back to the missing beat.

Actually, it was an extra beat come to think of it. My pumper throws an extra beat at odd intervals. To check it out the Doc wired me up to a little monitor complete with battery pack worn at the waist for 24 hours. Doc wanted to see if there was any irregularity connected with my daily routine.

I got to thinking. I'm a married man. And a marriage includes connubial bliss. So I got the idea I'd like to see how that little monitor performed when it got to record something worth spiking about. Actually, I thought I'd fry the circuits on that sucker.

As you can imagine, it took a lot of talking to get Maude to see it my way —advancement of science and all that. But after awhile she came around and we brought it off. Didn't even get tangled up in all those wires. It was a thrill.

Well, Sir. Back at the Doc's office the word got out and not only was the Doc interested in advancing science but he called in his nurse, naturally, and his secretary and the bookkeeper! It was like watching an Apollo rocket lift-off on television, everybody glomming their eyes on that monitor.

The Doc said, "roll'em" and the monitor started clicking its little paper record. Sure enough there were the sporadic odd beats jumping into the rhythm of the heartworks. Except when we reached the climax part, so to speak. There that little sucker hummed along nice as you please, never missing a beat for about two hours. The scientists were amazed.

You bet your boots I hustled home to Maude. In fact I remind her frequently about the health giving side effects of connubial bliss. But she sez without the wires and the little clicking noises it's not quite the same.

My heart attack took place up in Bozeman, Montana, after I announced to the group I was speaking to that I was having a heart attack and I went over and lay down on the floor to wait for the ambulance I wondered why everyone gathered around with an eager look in their eyes. Turns out this group had just finished a course on resuscitation. They were all waiting for me to pass out so they could jump down in my face to do their kiss of life thing.

Didn't happen.

A week later in the hospital I got this urge to write to everyone I knew. But really, you know, how much is there to tell about a heart attack? Actually it's pretty dull stuff to parties of the second part. So to entertain my friends I concocted this cockamamie story about the controls on my bed. You know, those controls where you punch a button and the bed goes up or down and folds in the middle. Well, I wrote my friends telling them of a new therapy. They connect those bed controls to your privates, yep. It goes up and down and even folds in the middle — all with the push of a button.

Talk about a thrill.

Saving A Dime

Listen up flatlanders. Oregon Bill's gonna show you how to save a dime on doctor bills. Yep. First, get yourself Triple A emergency road service. Then buy a Black and Decker circular saw. Here's the yarn.

Long time ago I had a heart attack up in Missoula, Montana. Scared the dickens out of me. So when I got back on my feet I started walking. Walked morning and night. Even got up to five miles a day. One day in the middle of a walk I up and jogged, real slow, from one telephone pole to the next, expecting at any minute that dull, throbbing, pain in my right shoulder. Didn't happen...so I kept on jogging.

Ran most every day for years except when I got a sciatic pain down my leg. Then I'd go back to walking, only I'd race-walk rolling my hips. It's crazy as hell to look at; your buns wagging back and forth the harder you walk. Got so the local log truckers couldn't hardly stand it and they'd blast me with their air horns. Well, I'm telling you I was a sight in my brief red shorts, buns wagging down the road.

I just blew those truckers a kiss in their rear view mirrors. Made 'em mad as hell.

Maude, though, she thought I was cute in a wiggly sort of way.

Any rate, back to saving money on doctor bills.

My doctor up and declared one day it was time to get some snap shots of the old pumper. You know, the kind where they slip a wire up a vein and into the heartworks. They shoot in a little dye then they take snapshots of the valves, pumps, and stuff.

Wouldn't you know the peek-a-boo sawbones in charge of the Polaroids comes up to me still lying on the table and says, "Bill, we're gonna cut on you. You've got three hoses to bring blood to the heart and your best hose is blocked 85 percent."

Well. They cut and I got the bill.

Whoooeee!

That started me thinking about how an ordinary Jack can save a dime on medical costs. My first recommendation is to buy an emergency road service policy. You know, like from Triple A.

You see, they first have to stop that heart in order to operate on it. Afterward, they have to jump start the blame thing. Now, most everything around my place needs to be jump started. Take Maude, for instance, she's not worth a damn until you slip her a little caffeine on rainy cold mornings. And my pickup is the same way. Only the pickup requires jumper cables not caffeine.

So I figured instead of letting the Docs bill you for using their fancy, chrome plated, electrical gee whiz to jump start your heart, why you could just phone AAA. Tell them to back up to the hospital window nearest the cutting room. Run the cables in through the window. Hit the accelerator to raise the amps. And connect her up on the positive and the negative.

Should be a piece of cake. Those heart muscles oughta twitch real steady.

Now, for my second recommendation — a Black and Decker circular saw.

I got this idea sometime after my operation, I was watching a medical video tape of heart by-pass surgery. I'll be damned if they didn't whip out what looked like a platinum plated circular saw. The Doc ran that baby right up the chest bone. Sternum I think they call it. Looked to me like they set 'er for about three quarters of an inch deep. Then, zzzruuup. I mean, it was slick.

But why wouldn't the old Black and Decker from the shop do just as good? Probably save you a nickel too. Oh sure, you'd have to wash the fool thing down good with grandma's lye soap. But who said saving money was easy for a working stiff.

The end of this yarn is a happy one. Old Bill made medical history. Yep. They was going to go in and perform triple by-pass surgery but I talked them into a fiver. Yes sir, Old Bill said, "Doc. I don't care how you hook up those first three veins but I want you to make two extras. Run one of 'em up to my brain. Run the other one down to my privates. A little extra circulation oughta help both organs."

Darn, if he didn't do it.

So today Old Bill is the only thinking woman's Romeo they've got here in Brownsville, Oregon. But then, Bill runs with the over sixty crowd. The competition is not all that much in either department.

Gets It Right

Well now, Oregon Bill is back in the hospital with another heart attack. Second one this year. Sez he's finally getting it right though. Here's the yarn.

Maude sez the old coot had a baby...a baby heart attack, that is. Bill and baby are doing fine and will be home in five days. After Bill learned he had a "baby" he called it an "immaculate infarction".

They measure heart attacks by enzymes in the blood given off by damaged tissue. A good honest thump-the-chest infarction gives off about a 600 or 800 enzyme count. This time Bill caught a 200 count. Like he sez, he's finally getting it right.

Course you have to allow for Bill's brain power or lack of it. It's a known fact he can't count to 21 unless his fly is open. As his pal Welcome Owsley sez, "It's a war of brains out there and most times Bill is low on ammunition."

Still an experienced hand like Bill is bound to latch onto something worth passing along. Get there fast is Bill's advice. They've developed new medicines called thrombolytics that dissolve blood clots and everything else, claims Bill. Sez that thrombo juice went right past his heart dissolving everything. Went right up to his brain. Maude, though, claims he wasn't ever all that swift in the first place. Sez he hasn't changed a damn bit in the smart department.

Get to the emergency room on the double cause you only got about a 4 maybe 6 hour window and then the damage has been done. Dissolving the clot doesn't help much after the downstream tissue has died.

Bill's style is to have his heart attacks right after midnight, that way the emergency room is kind of quiet so you don't have to take a number. Maude purely puts the pedal to the metal on the way in. Bill's so impressed he sez he's looking for a stock car he can put her in over to the Lebanon speedway. Sez the old girl has nerves of steel and the guts of a cat burglar.

But depression is way under rated, sez Bill. Claims a good low down don't shave, drool at the side of the mouth, fall asleep when someone's talking to ya, that kinda depression is just good old fashioned horse sense. Anyone who is cheerful after an infarction is both sick and dumb.

I mean you wouldn't give up steak and eggs while you wuz feelin good would you? No, sir. Nobody ever put out a good stogie while they wuz ahead of the game. You don't get up off the couch and pound the pavement on a rainy Oregon morning just because you wuz feelin swell. No, sir. You do things like that cause you're depressed real bad.

To live right as a heart patient you definitely have to be a little insane. A good heavy depression will get yer insanity off to a good start. Blue milk, raw carrots, and all that other good stuff they give cardiac rehab types, keeps the insanity goin nicely.

Bill had a 48 hour depression and then hung it up. Sez it got a little boring. Besides, Maude wouldn't put up with it.

So when the elephant sits on your chest, or, when that thrilling ache radiates down your arm, do just two things. Get over to the emergency room fast. Then, when things cool down insist on two days of crying in your beer.

Without the beer of course. I mean, if these lessons were easy to learn then everyone would be doing it.

The Achy Breaky Heart

Yeah, I know yer tired of news about Bill's heart attacks. Don't blame yuz. If it wasn't happening to me I'd be bored too. So all you sane and healthy people slide on back to the want ads section of this here newspaper. Buy yourself a Mercedes Benz confiscated in a government drug bust. The regular readers here, all the old gaffers around town as well as assorted riffraff, are going to unlax and relax while Bill flaps his lips about his heart works one more time.

But, technically speaking, Bill has a breaky heart not an achy one. That's why the Doc calls him "silent ischemic".

Actually when the Doc first called him that, Ol' Bill rared back to smack him one, Doc or no Doc. He figured "silent ischemic" was something folks did in private down in Youjean or up in Portland. But all the term means is that Bill's heart never aches; it just breaks…twice this year at about twelve thirty in the A.M. That's when Maude and Bill tore off for the emergency room in Corvallis roaring down the freeway in the middle of the night.

Most folks get an achy heart, a warning pain of some sort called "angina". It means the heart muscle isn't getting enough oxygen. But not Bill. He'll be going lickety split, feelin fine when all of a sudden he just busts out with a full blown infarction, a blockage along one of the arteries. In a little while a bit of heart muscle dies. Then Bill he gets seven days to admire nurses in the recovery room. No admiring is permitted in the emergency room at twelve thirty in the A.M.

But here's the real interesting news.

Bill's there in the E.R. answering questions like, "What's your Mother's maiden name, birthday, and social security number," while they pop nitroglycerin pills under his tongue, one, two, three.

No help. Damned if that left arm don't still radiate pain clear to the finger tips and the elephant still sits on the chest.

Then they start shooting him with morphine, one, two, three. They do this between questions like, "Bill, have you ever had ulcers?"

He's sitting there with three morphine shots to the bod and the arm still hurts a heap. Bill's thinking, "Three nitros, three morphines and no relief. I'm in a heap of trouble here." Then the emergency room Doc blurts right out of the blue, "Bill, you sure are calm!"

Well now that is a remarkable statement considering the circumstances. And it gives me a chance to put an idea in your skull. Let it roll around in there and tomorrow morning when you bend down to tie your shoes why that idea will slide forward and smack you on those there frontal lobes. Then, when you lie down in bed at night the same idea will roll back and whomp you on the brain stem, your reptilian brain, doncha know. That's good, cause this idea has gotta change your brain at a basic level.

So here's the idea: calmness can add up just like tension. You all know how you can get all wound up and frazzled over the orneriness of life. Well, it's the same with calmness. You can build it up…

Neat idea. Storing up calmness like a bank account. That's what you practice in an art called aikido. Bill and Maude are students of aikido. Next week Bill will tell you a little bit about the art. Next thing you know it you'll be able to amaze the Doc in the emergency room of your choice.

Three From The Heart

Ease back there. Relax and unlax. Your neighbor, Oregon Bill, is gonna teach. The old gaffer has had eighteen years of cardiac adventures and he's got something to say. So all you pupils straighten up and pay attention.

It all boils down to three questions. Yep, playing the cardiac game is only a matter of getting your head straight on these three questions:

1. Is it an event or a disease?
2. Who is in charge?
3. Is it a curse or a gift?

Take question number one, is it an event or a disease? Dumb question, right? Of course it's a disease! But, just between you, me and the fence post, it took like twelve years before I began to act like my heart attacks were a disease. Don't laugh! I ain't alone. Coronaries act like an event. That's why they call them heart "attacks".

Everything about that dull throbbing thrill in the arm, that elephant sitting on your chest screams wham, bam, something is a whole lot wrong here! Then it's over. Done. Finished. Or, so it seems.

You feel pretty weak, scared but fairly normal lying there in the hospital. All the parts are in one place and functioning about as usual. Some folks even skip seeing the Doc and only find out years later they had a "little" heart attack. Me? I have no angina (pain in the heart muscle cause it's not getting' enough oxygen) so it's easy to say, "Glad that's over, now I can get back to my life."

Other than feeling a little guilt it's real easy to go back to the couch to watch the toob, to go back to a big fat hamburger with extra order of fries. Easy as pie on Monday mornings to go back to push, push on the job and sweat the details. A whole lot of certified

All-American post-infarction males and females do just that. It's as right as apple pie a la mode.

Yep. Heart attacks are an event. Or, it seems like it.

Sure, the Doc tells you the standard stuff: "aspirin every day; exercise; skin off the chicken; stop smoking." Big deal. Well, maybe the coffin nails are a biggie but I wouldn't know about that. I smoked a pipe like a chimney stack for all of two weeks after my freshman year in college. When the girls didn't start seein' me as Ronald Coleman or some other slick movie star, I said to hell with it. Never smoked again.

Coronary disease plays right along with the act. The build-up of artery blocking deposits take a very long time and is so very silent. Oh, you might get a little breathy walking up the stairs but it's nothing a good night's sleep and a big bacon and egg breakfast won't cure! Right?

Wrong!

It ain't easy to remember what's plain as day to a Doc — coronary occlusions are a progressive, every-minute-of-every-day disease. Until that light goes on in your noggin, no way do you think serious about a changing' your life-style to put that damned disease in reverse.

Like I say, it took me twelve years to hear the question and then act like heart attacks are a disease, not an event. I mean, I ain't exactly a rocket scientist when it comes to figurin' things out. But stop by here next week and I'll tell you what I know about the other two questions.

Class dismissed. No homework tonight.

Cardiac Questions

Oregon Bill is gonna teach. The subject is cardiac adventures. Most of you males, and even some of you post-menopause women, will get a pop quiz on your heart health sooner or later. So listen up. Professor Bill has the subject boiled down to three questions. Last week he talked about the first one, is it an event or a disease? Here are the other two.

Who's in charge? It's real easy to be passive in your own care after a heart attack. Why is that? Well, mainly it's an unequal experience level. The Doc has seen more achy, breaky hearts than you have and he, or she, has fiddled around with a lot of them, sometimes with encouraging results. But you, you've got only one heart and precious little experience caring for it. So it's real easy to turn your heart's care over to the Doc.

But listen to this. The Doc's basic outlook is one of doing his or her best to extend out a little longer your slide down hill. The Doc usually doesn't think about halting the disease let alone reversing it. The essential medical problem is how to manage your case such that they flatten a few degrees off the down-hill slope, a pretty slippery one at that.

So if you are to reverse the disease, if you are going to make a comprehensive life-style change then you've got to become President of the Board. Get the best advice and most experienced Doc you can afford. Consult with the physician whole heartedly. But you make the decisions.

You see, it is well known on the wards and in the emergency rooms that the ornery ones, the demanding and assertive ones battle disease and injury a whole lot more effectively than do the sweet and the passive. The mild and unassertive slip away real easy.

Unless we accept the idea that we are responsible for our illness how can we take responsibility for our wellness? The thing that scares people off from seeing heart disease as reversible is the realization that they got themselves in trouble in the first place. It's mighty comfortable to put the Doc in charge of your heart because if you take control you gotta stare down two questions: what did I do wrong, and, how do I do right? And none of us likes to admit we messed up lying on the couch, bottling up all that stress, scarfing all that oily food, and smoking all them coffin nails.

But to put yourself in charge you first have to consider a dopey third question.

Is it a curse or a gift? Yeah, yeah I know. Sounds like Oregon Bill is a brick shy of a full load. You've got to be insane to think of a coronary occlusion as a gift. Many who get presents like this die on the spot. The other half have one foot on a banana peel. Some gift!

Let's come at it another way. Why is it human critters with emphysema keep light'n up one cigarette after t'other even when they've got an oxygen tank by their side? Human folks is wonderful contrary and stubborn ain't they. "I'll be damned if this affliction will change me…all it can do is kill me. Well piffle!"

But there is another way to think. You can think of heart disease as a gift. It's a wake-up call. It's a reminder to start living fully and well whatever time remains. For me, my heart attack (the third one, I don't catch on too quick) was the gift of a re-set button. It was also the gift of a new life with new pleasures and disciplines I never would have likely encountered otherwise - particularly yoga, meditation, or all vegetable meals. Finally, it was the gift of feeling my own feelings. Heart folks in general, you see, tend to wall off their feelings. So I learned that to heal your heart you must learn to open your heart.

Before you choose to change, to deliberately become a vegetarian, a walker, a meditator, to manage stress through meditation and yoga, to join a support group where you share your not always nice feelings — before you do any of these things you first have to choose to think of heart disease as a gift, not a curse.

Spring Plowing

One of the problems with growing old is that you run out of role models for the doing of it. Yep, one minute yer lookin up to certain old people, then before you know it yer lookin down at 'em....like six feet under. Got reminded of this problem when I started my spring plowing last week.

Started my spring plowing early, I did, and what with the winter rains and all, I got stuck — in about six inches of water. It all happened because I've been growing older of late. To be truthful I've been doing a mess of older growing of late. Ended up calling Rick's Towing to extract me from the furrow I'd plowed.

Here's the yarn.

Like every Tuesday, I'd hustled over to Corvallis to swill coffee and swap lies with a bunch of old geezers I us'ta work with. On the way back at noon, I fell asleep out on Seven Mile Lane just past the Glaser place and plowed into the ditch. It was the second time I'd pulled that there same trick and on the same road, about five years earlier, but a different field.

Not a scratch on me. Not a nick on my plowing machine, a Toyota pickup. Called the Morrow man and he yanked me back up on the road real slick. Whereupon I decided to have a little heart-to-heart talk with my doctor.

I tell the good doctor about my little adventure and he says, "Hummmm." Then he thumbs through my medical file and says, "Oops." And I yelled, "Wadda-ya-mean, oops!" "Well," he says, "your heart shows an ejection fraction of 35%. Below 50%," he continues, "most people begin to have trouble of some sort like angina, shortness of breath, swelling of the ankles, that sort of stuff." (Ejection fraction has to do with the squeeze efficiency of the heart.)

So I'm scheduled for an echocardiogram next week.

Next, the doctor asked me about snoring, quality of sleep and all like that there. Well, I've got plenty of sleep, partner, it's just the quality I'm low on. Like most men my age I'm up all night about every hour, so I seldom get into the R.E.M. sleep level. But this here is a family newspaper so I'll leave the getting up necessity to your imagination, dear reader. Suffice it to say, I'm scheduled for a sleep apnea test at mid-month.

What I'm getting at here is that growing old ain't for sissies. We all need a role model, like someone who has been there and managed their aging with a little spunk and grace. Take Welcome Owsley's brother Hambone. Now there is a model for how to manage the scary part of growing old.

That Hambone, he's a bigwig in the Indiana State Democratic Party. As a matter of fact, Ol' Hambone, he's the head of the whole she-bang. But of late he's been fighting the dickens out of prostate cancer. So wouldn't you know a professional friend of his, his Republican counterpart, he calls up Hambone to express his concern. And the Hambone man, he bellows out real loud, "Don't give my health problems a never-you-mind cause just today I rared back and joined the Republican Party." Well, Mr. Republican Chairman coughs and snorts before asking Hambone why he hauled off and did that so late in the game. "Well now," sez Hambone, "I couldn't abide the thought of my friends reading about the death of a good Democrat, but I didn't really give a damn if they read about some no-account Republican scoundrel biting the dust. So I just took myself down to the county court house, I did, and flat out changed over to the Republican Party. Respect for the bereaved you might call it."

Now there's a model I can roll with, Ol' Hambone Owsley, Welcome's brother.

Medical Frontier

Well now, as the faithful reader knows, Oregon Bill fell asleep at the wheel out on Seven Mile Lane couple of weeks ago. His doctor arranged for him to do a sleep study over to Good Samaritan Hospital. And Bill, he hot-footed it back to this particular frontier of medical science just to keep the Greater B'ville metro up to speed.

Sleep apnea test its called, and you spend the whole night doing it at the hospital. Snoring (among other things) is what gets you there to be tested. Seems like when you sleep the muscles and stuff at the back of the mouth and top of the throat start to relax. Air passing over the relaxed, flabby flesh produces a sound we call *snoring*. But when the relaxation goes too far, it shuts off the air passages completely, resulting in the lungs not doing their oxygen exchange thingy. Then somewhere in your brain, a neon "yikes" sign goes on and your body automatically snorts and jerks, which reestablishes muscle tone. Air-exchange resumes for a short while. Then you do the whole sequence over again. It can get so bad your wife will elbow your ribs forcefully and announce in your ear: "Breathe, you old goat! You stopped breathing."

They begin the sleep test by wiring you up. They glue (yes, glue) five wire monitors to your scalp, hair and all. Then they tape 3 or 4 wire leads to your jaw and upper lip. Next, they add a probe up both nostrils, The heart gets monitored by a couple of leads. Finally, leads are put on both legs. Oh yeah, the skin at each lead site is sorta lightly sandpapered to give good contact.

They plug all the leads, 25 or 30, into a box on the wall and say, "Now, lie down and sleep on your back."

Well, I never sleep on my back. Plus the sciatica in my left leg chooses that exact time to make life miserable. The restlessness and pain goes on until 2 or 3 in the morning, when they tell me they have enough readings. They stop the study right there and start the therapy, which is air pumped up the snozzola for the rest of the night.

The next morning, the technician tells me that during the test sequence I averaged about 30 apnea episodes an hour, and the oxygen saturation in my blood dropped to 83% (above 90% is normal). After they hooked me up to the air pump in the nose, all the apnea stopped and I achieved a 96% oxygen saturation in the bloodstream. Interestingly enough, I didn't have to use the bathroom after they started inflating me. That's what it is, a mild inflation of mouth and throat which keeps the air passages open. The pressure per square inch required varies from person to person, so I guess you could go up to Jerry's Rocket Fuel up on the highway and stick an air hose into your mouth to gauge what you need. When your eyes bug out, you are properly inflated, more or less.

Among other things, sleep apnea is related to high blood pressure. A drop in oxygen saturation, I guess, tells the pumper to work harder. Personally, I have been fighting high blood pressure for the last 25 years, resulting in a moderately enlarged left ventricle, which is the first step on the march to congestive heart failure.

Interestingly, too, sleep apnea is related to kidney function. When the kidneys don't get a chance to rest, they throw off a substance called A.C.E., which tells all the valves in the system to tighten up which in turn raises blood pressure. That's why a whole family of blood pressure medicines is called "A.C.E. inhibitors".

So, the sleep apnea therapy, as I say, means you get slightly inflated through a mask over the nose. If you don't watch it at night, you can begin to sort of hover a few inches above the mattress, inflated as you are. Every once in awhile, Maude has to reach out, grab my air hose, and pull me back down on the bed. Says she wouldn't bother with the fool contraption, except that when I'm drifting around the room, I take the covers with me.

The Thrills Continue

A s you know, dear reader, I had a heart attack up at church recently, and the thrill of open heart surgery following that. All I've got to say, though, is that I'm really fortunate to have inherited fighting genes because I've spent most of my life fighting my genes! Genetically my body wants to clog up the plumbing, most especially around the heart.

The bottom line is that I'm at home, I have three new vein grafts in the heart. I have an implanted pacemaker/defibrillator, and a 35% ejection fraction. The latter is dicey.

About the dice: An ejection fraction (the squeeze efficiency of the heart muscle) of 90% is normal. If you drop below 40%, the heart tends to throw in extra beats to make up for its lack of efficiency. Therefore, they implanted a pacemaker/defibrillator just like the one Dick Cheney has. Funny thing, too; I've begun sympathizing with our vice-president on the issue of drilling for oil in Alaska. What's a few thousand caribou or Eskimos? We need that oil, dang it!

Three positives: I've got three things going for me to improve the ejection fraction. First, they found sufficient vein "tubing" and sites to install three bypass grafts. The increased blood flow should restore strength to compromised heart muscle regions. Second, they have a new blood thinning agent called Coreg, which seems to show great promise in restoring pumping capacity in heart muscle. Finally, my history of vigilant cardiac self-care (diet, exercise, and stress reduction) is exemplary. In fact, that history of self-care is very likely one of the reasons I am still alive.

And a Giggle: My poor abused and insulted heart went into fibrillation (quivering instead of pumping) twice in the hospital, once before and once after the open-heart procedure. When the first event happened, unknown to me, the reacting team on the floor had been watching for it. I'd been throwing extra beats all day, but those had not yet become a long string of irregular beats. When it finally arrived in the early evening, I remember twisting in bed and exclaiming, "Something is wrong!" I felt myself entering a long red tunnel, the same tunnel I had first experienced during the heart attack at church. Bingo, the response team filled the room and they shocked me on the chest with paddles.

My impression is that the shock threw me three feet into the air, returning my heart to normal rhythm. Coming back down as I hit the bed on the first bounce, I exclaimed loudly to the whole response team, "My, you do good work!"

The whole floor is still giggling, I'm told.

Assisted Living

We all dread the idea of being placed in a care facility in our last years of life, don't we now? Not having a car, using a walker, enduring the faint smell of urine in the long hallways, forced joviality of visitors, all of these are not the best feature of our "golden years", not by a long shot. Yet, in a strange sense, each and every one of us is already enrolled in an assisted living program and I have been for years. It's called "my life". The care facility housing us is called "planet Earth". Here is how I know.

Oregon Bill's heart arrested recently. First they pounded on his chest. Then they reared back and hit him with the electric shock paddles. Brought the old gaffer's pumper right around sure enough. Then they hauled off and planted a titanium unit the size of a small cigarette pack in the chest, just under the skin with wires running down into the heart chambers. That thingamabob is a defibrillator and a pace-maker. It makes "paces" about ten percent of the time. That pace making activity fills me with both a sense of wonder and a sense of dread all at the same time. That dread arises when I acknowledge that my living is now assisted, assisted by an electronic widget that could fail as human contrivances are prone to do. The sense of wonder arises when I acknowledge that I've always had an electronic beat mechanism, even a back-up system, functioning steadily in my heart all my born days — a kind of *assisted living* feature built into my body and yours.

I deal with the feelings of fear and dread when they arise as best I can. Mainly, I cope by calling to mind another feature of assisted living here on planet Earth, a feature called love. We all begin life, do we not, in an assisted living facility called a womb. After we are discharged from that facility we begin the lifetime task of seeking and building a community around us to cushion the snares and pain that is our lot, as well as to celebrate the good times when they roll. In a very real sense we all have to build our very own *care facility* to assist us in living out our lives.

Maude and me felt ourselves lifted and carried through the whole cardiac event by our community. We were held in the light in an activity called prayer. My eldest son captured the image and feeling of those prayers one evening in the hospital when he remarked, "Dad, this whole room just glows from the light of those prayers."

In addition to light, prayer also takes the form of energy. Our friends cleaned our house, brought food, mowed the yard, fed the pets, housed Maude near the hospital, took care of the orchard, transported us home, brought healing music and Reiki; brought their energy to the hospital and later to our home. Energy freely, lovingly given is also a form of prayer.

How do I know? I've been there. How can you know? Try using assisted living as a lens to look at your own circumstance; the events you call your life here on planet Earth. How is your life assisted?

Busting Out of Prison

Who me?

Material: found cast iron, 27" height, 16" width, 16" depth

Owner: Artist

Humboldt Boy

The faithful reader of this here column knows full well that Oregon Bill is a fraud seeing as how he was raised on a redwood stump down there in Eureka, California. He's no more an Oregonian than Arnold Schwartzenegger. Imagine my surprise then to learn about a world-renown artist who lived the last third of his life in Humboldt County and I knew nothing about the bloke. Zip.

The Maude girl and I zipped down to the U of O last week to hear a New York art critic, Wolf was his name, lecture on the Morris Graves paintings held in the museum there. Morris Graves, you see, is the Humboldt boy about whom I was ignorant. What follows here is a review of the Graves career and then I'll tell you about the line that knocked me clean off my redwood stump.

Graves was born here in Northwest Oregon actually, in the year 1910. So he is 20 years my senior. He began his artistic career in Seattle where he resided for many years but visited Japan early on. He never recovered from the artistic and natural aesthetic he encountered there. Many of those early paintings began as elaborately complex, intricate backgrounds on which with a few bold, often slashing strokes, he'd place a striking figure or symbol in the foreground. Much of this work was spiritually evocative.

Graves, always socially reclusive, then pulled up stakes and took himself off to Ireland where he continued what he called his *religious studies* — those spiritually evocative paintings.

He died just a few years ago in Humboldt County where he'd spent the last third of his ninety-year life. He retreated to a lake there surrounded by redwoods. Wolf, the art critic, told us that in his Humboldt years Graves turned away from his religious studies in his painting and took up the flower as his subject. Wolf ranks him as one of the two best artists ever at interpreting the presence of the flower.

As you would expect, a ninety-year productive career in art yields a raft of paintings, probably well into the thousands. With that prodigious a body of work Wolf had to ask Graves the obvious question: "Which ones are the best?" To which Morris Graves gave this stunning reply: "Oh, there are only 5 or 6 real paintings there; the rest were done by Morris Graves!"

Yes! That's my Humboldt boy. He spoke directly to the soul of this Grizzly Creek, Eel River bar scalawag now grown old and grizzled. You see, for years I've known that whatever my soul might be it is not my brain, nor my ego, nor, certainly, this particular body. Our egos tell us we are separate and apart from all else. No one can die our death. Our ego tells us to feel secure because this separate self has gathered all the stuff money will buy; to feel puffed up when praised; to take revenge when wronged or at least go off and sulk; to compete against all comers in this dog-eat-dog world. And so on and on. That is the work of our ego. Our soul's work is to recognize this about ourselves then lurch toward an alternative identity. In Christianity it is called becoming a disciple. Becoming a disciple means dying to a certain identity, such as being Morris Graves, so that the real paintings can get born in this life here and now.

Little Me

There is a space between birth and death that each of us calls *my life*. In that space, we try to figure out how did this *me* get here, what is this me supposed to do, and whence will this *me* return when its heart thumps its last thump? It's our soul work, isn't it now?

Meanwhile, we are born into a world we did not make, and that world presses in on us as we scramble around trying to form a *self*. We use duct-tape, bailing wire and twine to cobble together the pieces — a habit here, an obstinacy there, a whole lot of gender awareness, plus down-home ethics, a little Sunday school theology, and perhaps a dash of anger or rebelliousness. We call that assemblage *me*. It's our sense of self apart and separate from everything and everyone else in the universe.

The rare epiphanies that enter our lives raise questions about that little *me* there inside my skin. It happened to me while meditating. Suddenly, I knew that whatever my soul might be, it was not that chattering monkey-brain up there compulsively running its tapes. Meditating again the next night, I realized that every bit of that brain chatter was ego related — yadda, yadda, yadda, about looking wise, being kind, being firm, looking good, looking sexy, being funny, and so on, and on, and on. If meditation was a route to knowing my soul, then I'd have to get past the ceaseless ego chatter rattling around in my skull.

Told my pal Welcome Owsley about that little epiphany of mine, and he allowed as how I wasn't as bad off as some folk. "Shoot, Bill," sez Owsley. "There's folks around that can't get in touch with anything deeper than muscle and gristle. They confuse their soul with the prettiness or the plainness of the body they walk around in."

Some help, that Owsley. But I did find help in Sue Kidd's book, "The Dance of the Dissident Daughter".

It's a slog, though; I Kidd you not. Sue Kidd, a married mother of two, thirty something, a nationally recognized religious writer of the Baptist persuasion, awoke to her patriarchal world and it made her mad as hell. But while the anger is honest and compelling enough, this is not a book about rage. It's a book about a search for one's soul while living as an alien on a planet controlled by men — Planet Earth. I call her work a "slog" only because she lives such a richly textured, complex, creative inner life it's tough on the male attention span. The pages add up relentlessly as she unravels the fine detailed progression of her spiritual journey.

Truth is, we men might not be able to get there from here. Testosterone, you know. Take off the cover of a man's emotional control panel and you find only two buttons. One is green, the other is red. But take the cover off a woman's emotional control panel, and you find a wondrous complexity of rheostats, microchips, transistors, and goodness knows what else. Men, we have little hope of ever understanding the full richness of her inner life.

For example, Kidd learns to make deliberate and ever more daring use of ritual and symbolism to both affirm and to deepen a spiritual awareness uncovered on her journey. The only bloke I know that works the same territory is the poet Robert Bly with his male drumming circles. Alongside Kidd, though, Bly comes off timid and unimaginative. But, then, "it takes ovaries", says Kidd.

So, if you are mucking around the messy work of trying to come to know your own soul and asking yourself to live that knowing, then Kidd's journal is your kind of book.

Prison Life

I have had 30 years experience dealing first with heart adventures and then with diabetes. During those years, I met a lot of people trying to care for their heart and blood sugar by eating right, exercising, and reducing stress. Some succeeded. A lot failed. Failure, or the sabotaging of our own good health, I've concluded, is connected to the problem of soul work. Here's my thinking.

Two years ago I had some small-engine work done here in Brownsville. One year later I returned with another engine problem. "Sorry Bill," sez the mechanic, "I don't do engine work anymore. Diabetes has wrecked my eyes. I can't see things up close."

"Well now," sez I. "Sorry to hear that. But, as it turns out, you are in luck. We're having our monthly diabetes/cardiac support group meeting at our church up in Sweet Home tonight. I'll pick you up."

"Sorry," he shoots back. "I don't do groups."

"Prisoner," I thought. Each one of us builds our own ego prison, don't we now, brick by brick. Here's a guy going blind and help is just outside his prison walls. But he can't get there from here.

Like I say, I've had 30 years experience at the game. And I've met a ton of cardiac/diabetic people. Many, perhaps most, make a gesture toward changing their diet. A few exercise sporadically. But almost nobody, in my experience, gets systematic about stress reduction. Why is this? Why do people imprison themselves in a life-style that jeopardizes their health? And why are these self-constructed ego prisons so effective? Even the scared spitless can't escape. And the strong-willed slack off after awhile; then find themselves back behind bars of their own making. Then we all turn to the doctor pleading for the magic get-out-of-prison pill. Why is this?

I've come to the conclusion the problem is in feeding the soul. You can't solve your ego prison problem by attacking the walls and bars head-on. You've got to first feed your soul. Because, you see, down deep you doubt that you are worth all that trouble.

To come to know you are worth the price of breaking out of your own ego prison, I believe you first have to feed your soul. Friends of mine walk on an Oregon beach to put themselves in touch with the infinite. My daughter feeds her soul by rocking and walking babies at a women's shelter. If gardening allows you to experience the renewing power and beauty of the universe, do that. If music and art allow you to glimpse the unseen and to align yourself there, then participate wholly. If a walk in an Oregon forest or by an Oregon stream speaks deeply to you, then go listen. Feed your soul however you can. But feed your soul.

Me? I choose to go to church. But, then, left to my own devices I often fail to feed my soul. I lean toward spiritual laziness when alone. I need a community to find and maintain my path out of my ego prison.

Hush now, I'm thinking. I'm thinking about the import of it all.

Yadda, Yadda, Yadda

Actually this here column is a bit too personal, too close to the bone for comfortable reading. Moreover, it is a bit abstract and religious, not everybody's cup of tea. So maybe, dear reader, you might want to skip back to the editorials and let Editor Don raise your blood pressure and get you to muttering to yourself.

Meanwhile the rest of us are going back to the Age of Enlightenment and earlier.

Descartes, it was, who asked himself the plain question, "Is there anything I can know with absolute certainty?" His answer became the famous dictum, "I think therefore I am." Descartes realized that the fact that he was always thinking was beyond doubt and so he equated *thinking* with *being*. It wasn't until 300 years later that Jean-Paul Sarte asked his uppity questions, "But, Monsieur Descartes, who is it that realizes the thinker is thinking?" Sarte then went on to assert, "The consciousness that says 'I am' is not the consciousness that thinks." What did he mean by that?

Well, if there were nothing but thought in you, you wouldn't even know you were thinking. You would be like the dreamer who doesn't know he is dreaming . When you know you are dreaming you are awake within the dream. Similarly, when you are awake to the fact that the incessant talk in your head is not who you ultimately are, another level of consciousness comes into play.

The sad human truth is that the incessant talk in your head is your ego doing its yadda, yadda, yadda thing. We mistake that voice in the head for who we really are — a consciousness in sync with the universe.

So what does all this fancy talk have to do with me? Well, for a year now I've been a part of a study group engaged in materials entitled "Becoming A Disciple through Bible Study". I've come to the conclusion you can't get there from here. Yes, Bible study is illuminating, moving even, but becoming a disciple I've come to believe involves coming to terms with your ego — the illusory chatter filling the brain so insistently. We think it must be the real me. It ain't.

Jesus, it is reported, said, "I am the way, the truth, and the life." Jesus speaks here of the innermost I am, the essential identity of all human kind. He speaks to the life that you are. Some Christian mystics have called it the Christ within. Buddhists call it your Buddha nature. Hindus call it the Atman, the in-dwelling God. When you are in touch with the dimension within yourself all your actions will reflect the oneness with life that you sense deep within.

They say the ego is a terrible master but a wonderful servant. And so I see my path to discipleship as a matter of becoming ego-aware and coaxing it toward servant-hood. It is a matter of breaking out of the ego prison walls I have so lovingly erected brick by brick as I was born into a family, became part of a community, lurched toward gender identity, etc., etc., etc.

All of those ideas are brilliantly new, of course. Well, not exactly. Possibly they were fresh in the 14th century when Hafiz, the Sufi poet wrote: "I am the hole in the flute that the Christ's breath moves through. Listen to the music."

There you have it. Don't say I didn't warn you. Like I say, it's a bit close to the bone.

Servant and Master

Growing old is so absurd. The treachery of an aging body does, however, serve a purpose. The treachery bashes the ego so mercilessly you are forced to look more closely at the thing you call the *self*. Take me and summer steelheading for starters. Now, there's a yarn.

Time was I waded pretty aggressively fly fishing for summer steelhead on the Siletz, Umpqua or Deschutes Rivers. Then last summer this 77-year-old man's ego got bonked big time fishing the Grande Ronde. Took my little self down to the bank of that river, I did, and promptly fell in. Floated off in the current (waders are buoyant if you've cinched them up tight enough), then hit a rock, righted myself and waded ashore with only 4 inches or so of water in my waders. Walked up the river a ways and waded back in. But the boulders there were slick as snot and I found myself trying out for the swimming team once more. This time, however, my son came out of nowhere, grabbed me by the nap of the neck and got me out of the fast water and onto shore. For the next hour or so I fished just that way — my son holding his kitten (me) by the nap of the neck until I talked him into letting me down. He agreed to this only after I promised him I'd fish in water no deeper than my ankles.

What a revolting development. And hard on the ego too — that identity I'd fashioned over time using a lot of gender stuff given to me growing up in the country; added a few prejudices and habits from the same source; incorporated a streak of independence as well as a mélange of copy-cat stuff from the movies, Sunday School, my gang, popular music, and so forth. All these repeated expressions, choices, habits, and preferences slowly became that stable ego entity that goes by the name *me* or *myself* or *I*. The insult of growing old however invites you to consider making that ego a servant instead of a master. That's the spiritual task of aging, you know, to encompass your ego such that it no longer automatically dictates an angry, petulant, or bravado response to life's foibles. It's nature's way of helping you attend to self-work yet undone.

Thich Nhat Hanh in his book <u>Living Buddha, Living Christ</u> has an interesting take on this ego awareness task of ours. Hanh asserts that the Christian idea of salvation and the Buddhist idea of enlightenment are not that far apart. He thinks of the two traditions as complementary modes of moving from our natural self centeredness (that ego problem again) to re-centering in a higher order of existence, that is: in compassion, kindness, generosity, forgiveness, and justice. My shorthand name for that re-centering process is to call it, "making the ego your servant not your master." The body growing old is simply nature's way of convening that seminar.

Castrating An Ego

All right campers, what we've got here is a summary of nine months work plus a smart-alecky poem. Both the poem and the work are about learning to walk *the path*.

First, the work.

Three questions dominated my nine months as a part of a group using materials entitled "Becoming A Disciple Through Bible Study". These questions arose on day one; they continued all through the year and remain with me now.

Question One: What is the ineffable entity we spell G-O-D? The ineffable is beyond words but the words I use to describe G-O-D, those words shape how I pray, how I worship, how I live my life. Is the ineffable a super Santa Claus or more like an infinite energy field? What do I mean by the word God? Or, is ours a universe made up of matter only and devoid of meaning?

Question Two: Where is God in this collection of documents called the Bible? Is this the word of God, inerrant and absolute? If the Bible is inerrant and absolute, how do I resolve its internal curiosities, discrepancies, and contradictions? Or is this collection of documents, a record of a desert culture in the Mideast struggling powerfully to come to know and to be in a relationship with God? If it is the latter, what do I do with the gospels and writings suppressed by the church after the Council of Nicea and just recently discovered at Nag Hamadi?

Question Three: How do I get there from here? Becoming a disciple is more than a head-trip, more than being able to cite the Bible chapter and verse. For me right now that *more* is the struggle to become ego-aware and to make that ego of mine a servant not my master. Christ counseled we must die to our ordinary selves. I continue my path toward discipleship by striving to examine my *ordinary self* using Ekart Tolle's book, <u>A New Earth</u>.

The ego, you know, is the identity each of us puts together. A little string, duct-tape, and bailing wire holds the whole jerry-built assemblage in place. We call that assemblage *me*. It is our prison; a rather comfortable prison but a prison nonetheless. Busting out, that is, *dying to our ordinary self* is a formidable task. Hafiz, a 14th Century poet beloved in Persia, has some cheeky observations about this prison break-out problem that confronts you and me.

Castrating An Ego

The only problem with not castrating
A gigantic ego is
That it will surely become enormous
And father
A hundred screaming ideas and kids
Who will then all quickly grow-up
And skillfully proceed
To run up every imaginable debt
And complication of which your brain
Can conceive
This would concern normal parents.
And any seekers of freedom
And the local merchants nearby as well.
They could very easily become forced
To disturb your peace;
All those worries and bills could turn to
Wailing ghosts.
The only problem with not lassoing
A runaway ego is
You won't have much desire to sing
In this sweet, sweet
World.

Unused Capacity

As the faithful reader knows, Oregon Bill has a pacemaker/defibrillator sewn into his chest with wires running down into the heart chambers. But, that electronic device is only required to make paces ten percent of the time because his heart still beats correctly nine times out of ten. So, ninety percent of that contraption's pace-making capacity is unused. Bill figures he could make big bucks if only he could devise a way to export paces from his body to yours. Hey, don't laugh! When your body gets to where it needs a timely pace or two, you'll fork over serious dollars for Bill's remote-origins-paces.

Well now, that silly reverie about my pacemaker's unused capacity got me to thinking about other parts of my life. Where else in that life am I getting by with just a ten percent output? The answer, dear hearts, is play. I do precious little of it. I play very little in the earnest, material world of work, goals, and accomplishments. I play even less in the spiritual world of mystery, awe, and transcendence. But I have been helped in that latter realm, the spiritual one, by a church, if you can imagine that.

"Nuts for Jesus" is what we do in that church. We harvest, dry, package, and sell nuts to support "Manna", a free meal every Friday for the hungry. Wearing a badge that identifies you as one of the Nuts for Jesus helps keep a giggle in your heart as well as a certain lightness in your being. Both qualities, giggles and lightness, are good for play.

Nikki is a resident wise woman in our community. Last week she announced she was doing God's work. "Yes," said Nikki: "When I moved into my house I discovered my two neighbors fiercely disliked one another. But now, after two or three years, they are firmly bonded. Their bond is the belief that I'm the weirdest neighbor they have ever had. Clearly, my weirdness is benevolent."

Transcendence, rising up and going beyond, is evident in Nikki's whimsical observation. Most of us are trapped in the identity, the "me", we've pasted together over a life time. By making fun of the self, that identifying weirdness of hers, Nikki signaled she was not trapped spiritually.

Recently, our community bid a playful goodbye to Howard, who succumbed to a long struggle with heart failure. Only two years ago he had been a stalwart dishwasher every Friday at the Manna meal. At the service for Howard the choir reworked the old hymn, "Just a Closer Walk with Thee" to belt out a revised, *"Just a Cleaner Wash for Thee"* as a sincerely whimsical farewell for brother Howard.

We also bid farewell to Glen, a severely retarded man, who never missed a Sunday worship service because he especially loved communion where he could loudly and lustily slurp the juice he was offered. So, naturally, we included the communion ritual in his memorial service because then, as we were instructed, we could all slurp long and lovingly in memory of Glen.

Every other week or so our pastor April grabs her guitar and we all join in on our theme song whose first line is, "Ours is the church where everyone is welcome; I know it's true 'cause I got through the door..."

So I am trying on this idea — perhaps we are fully human when we truly are at play. And perhaps our spiritual purpose is to be fully human right here, right now. Because you see, true play is defined as that which is done for its own sake only — no goals, no objectives, no payoffs, no heaven, no salvation. Play is a spiritual practice. Your playful self, like mine, may be a largely unused capacity.

Let me put it another way. My sister Yvonne lived for a year at a YWCA while at college. Her chums early on referred to one another as "playmate." After graduation they continued to telephone playmate, to write playmate, to visit playmate, and to eventually bury playmate. What I wonder is this: What if you adopted Jesus as your playmate? What would that act mean for your spiritual world? How would you and playmate carry on right here, right now?

Adults at play

dult play happens here in Brownsville down at the Corner Café at least once a year, sometimes even twice or three times. The most recent occasion was the local inaugural ball celebrating our new president taking office. The ladies danced. Oh sure, a man or two joined them on the dance floor intermittently. But, mainly it was the ladies out there on the floor singly or with one another, moving, laughing, and bouncing to the rhythm of the music that gave expression to the joy of the evening. The ladies were at play.

In his book, <u>Play</u>, Stuart Brown describes the properties of play making it clear it is not merely a certain kind of activity but rather a state of mind. In his book he describes how play-states-of-mind (1) changes the brain, (2) opens the imagination, and (3) invigorates the soul. It's that last part, the soul vigor of play that interests me the most. But let's start first with listing a few qualities of adult play. Then we'll get to the soul work.

We've all participated in games that weren't playful at all. They were fierce competitions in which everyone was hell-bent on winning. Yes, competitive games are satisfying, engrossing, even rewarding but they are not play. Play is done for its own sake only. The "prize", the "winning", and the "score" are in the play itself. Play is its own reward. Moreover, play has a timeless quality. If you have ever asked the question, "Where did the time go?", you may have been at play. At play we are open to chance, to new moves, and new strategies. Improvisation is a strong quality in the play-state-of-mind. Play is also fun of course. It's inherently attractive. It's also voluntary. Play can never be an obligation, a duty or an assignment. (Though the human critter is ingenious in devising ways to make even the mandatory playful.) Nor do you want to stop. Play evokes a desire to continue. Finally, people at play worry less and less about how they look — dumb or smart, polished or awkward, athletic or klutzy. At play we are content to look goofy. Acting goofy is a deliberate diminution of the ego. As the faithful reader knows, ego diminution is a huge part of Bill's spiritual work. Christ's injunction, remember, is to give up our ordinary lives, to surrender our precious selfhood, and to follow him. Therefore, this play business interests me because of its powers for illuminating one's ego and its dictates.

Joseph Campbell in his book <u>Myths of Light</u> writes that in the Japanese language, "There is a form of very polite discourse known as 'play language' (asobase kotoba) where instead of saying, 'I see you have come to Tokyo,' one says, 'I see that you are playing at being in Tokyo.'" The idea is that people do what they do voluntarily, as in a game. Play and drama have counterparts in Hindu theology as well, though not in their spoken language. Campbell admires this Eastern philosophy where what has to be done in this life you do with such will that you play at life. This leads Campbell to his widely quoted admonition, "Participate joyfully in the sorrows of life."

Oregon Bill had a talk with his ownself just the other day using, of course, asobase kotoba, the super polite Japanese language form. He said to himself, "Bill, I see you are playing at being in Brownsville." And it could have been true if only he'd gotten out there and joined the ladies on Joe's dance floor last January.

⊚n The Path

Phillipi III

Material: found cast iron, 64" height, 5" width, 33" depth
Owner: Artist

On the Path

My pal Welcome Owsley is always asking me, "Bill, what's your path? Is it skinny like a rat's tail or big enough for a natural man?"

You see, Welcome is a man of stern principles and always knew exactly what his life goal was — to become the town rake.

As Welcome says, "Life is one man gettin hugged for sneakin a kiss 'n another getting slapped. Besides, every town has gotta have one. Sorta puts you on the map to have a good rascal on the ramble."

Welcome got off to an early start, what with the name his father hung on him — Karl Marx Owsley (Welcome is a family nickname). Now that might not seem like much in these days. But you only have to go back to the 50s to remember what a bogeyman communism was. I mean you looked under your bed every night before you said your prayers afraid that one of those godless pinkos would grab your young mind and warp it in un-American ways.

Old Buckshot Owsley, young Karl Marx's dad, believed anarchists, like the Wobblie's, would have taken over the country during the Great Depression of the 30s if we hadn't passed the progressive income tax law. And the old bird might have been right.

Buckshot himself was a man of principle. Got himself canned as a foreman during those depression years for sticking up for his men, the work they did, and for the mean wages they took home. After he got the can tied to his tail, he hooked on as a chaser on the landing crew where my Uncle Cletus was the hook tender. Sat back to watch his little Karl Marx, Welcome, set out on his life path.

Except that Welcome got side tracked for a while when he was 10 or so. Thought he'd become a gaucho down in the Argentine. But after just one school year he gave up that gaucho stuff and came back to his true callin — becoming the town rake.

"Bill, you just can't chase two rabbits," Welcome said at the time. Like I said, when you are truly called you have to lead a life of principle. One of Welcome's principles is that "Mother nature is horny". "Bill," he'd poke me, "wake up! Look around. The universe is just dripping with hormones. Think what that means man."

Well, I thought about it of course. I mean even good old Jimmy Carter had a little lust in his heart. But after I mentioned it to Maude as casual and offhanded as I could, why all hell broke loose.

Started to eat out for awhile after that . Flying dishes unsettles a man's appetite.

Being a man of principle ain't no easy path.

It seems to me though, that to live a life of principle it helps to have a hero or two, what city dudes call *role models*. Welcome's main man is <u>Zorba the Greek</u>. I think Welcome reads that book at least two or three times a year. For about three months afterward he's a wonder. You can always tell, I mean, ALWAYS TELL when Welcome has got a fresh shot of insight about the responsibilities in being the town's certified rake.

But that inspiration can come from the damndest places. Why one afternoon and evening down at the Brownsville Tavern, Welcome quoted from <u>The Tibetan Book of the Dead</u> non-stop for two hours. Then the gang at the pool table decided Welcome and I were not fit company for no self-respecting tavern. So Welcome and I hightailed it outa there.

Oregon Bill might yet become an apprentice rake about town. But, confidentially, between you and me, he probably oughta find some other rabbit to chase.

On the Ball

Old timers in Japan talk about the three gifts: the sword, the mirror, and the ball. The sword represents the gift of power and the mirror is the gift of reflection or insight. But, the ball? Why it's the gift of resurgence and flexibility. A ball is always upright. You can never knock a ball down. Moreover, a ball can move in any direction. It can change course infinitely.

That image always brings to mind Bart Spinas because a ball he wasn't. Spinas was a tough, old time woods boss for a big outfit down on the coast. Ol' Bart logged a long time ago when they used oxen to pull logs to the water, or later, to railroads, using a skid road.

In those days they "sniped" every log. That is, a pair of axemen would cut off a slant at the butt end of the log so it would drag without catching the cross ties, tearing up the skid road. Bart's crew of ox drivers would hitch oxen to those sniped logs and slide them down to the landing. It was a main-strength-and-awkwardness show but it got the job done. And ol' Spinas purely loved the steady brute strength of those oxen especially when they bowed their neck and settled into a humongous load. Now, the owner of Bart's outfit was a forward looking feller. One day he showed up at the railroad landing with a new fangled Dolbeer Donkey. That Dolbeer Donkey, a steam engine sitting on a sled and driving a set of large spools of steel cable, was going to revolutionize logging here in the Northwest. But not on Bart's show. No sir rebob.

Just as soon as the owner went down the tracks on the speeder, Bart ordered his crew to hitch up the oxen to the new machine and drag it off into a gulch. Had a pair of fallers drop the biggest damned tree he could find right on top of the brand new Dolbeer Donkey. Mashed her down flatter than a pancake. Satisfied, Spinas went back to loggin with oxen just like his father had and just like the good Lord intended.

No sir, when Bart Spinas bowed his neck you knowed he was going to plow a mighty deep furrow right straight ahead come hell or high water. A ball of infinite flexibility he warn't.

Oregon Bill it turns out has a lot of Bart Spinas in him. Gets irritated, or just plain mad when something or someone interferes with his agenda. Why I've seen him jump off his tractor and bash it with a shovel when the fool thing wouldn't start on a cold morning. Even gets grumpy with Maude when she lays out a string of honey-dos after breakfast. That's probably why the flow gums up in Bill's heartworks. Type A personality, doncha know.

About a month ago Bill made a hellava discovery though. For about three years now Bill has been trying a breathing meditation. He sits "seiza" on his knees with his lower back as straight as he can keep it. Then he takes in a long slow breath through the nose. As he exhales slowly he extends "Ki" or life energy and lets his breath ride on the Ki to the ends of the universe. Does this daily for about twenty minutes. Says it coordinates his mind and body.

Well, a while ago Bill was talking with his Ki instructor about his agenda problem — getting irritated or angered so easily at frustrations. And the instructor says, "Yes, I noticed the same problem in myself. I was getting irritated when our new baby cried every morning just as I started meditating. So I thought about it and decided it was a problem of "tendo setsu" (sending Ki in one direction) versus "chido setsu" (sending Ki in infinite directions). Now, when I meditate I'm careful to send Ki infinitely in all directions. When the baby cries, I stop meditating and attend to him. I've already sent Ki in that direction. I can deal with it."

I don't know about the balky Massey Ferguson tractor out at Bill's place these days but Maude says Bill is a different man to live with. Says she's whomping up some prodigious honey-do lists just to test this Ki business.

Bill just grins and says, "Piece of cake. I've already sent plus Ki in that direction. I can deal with it."

Outa Puff

Welcome Owsley is reading some weird books these days. Yep. He's all bug-eyed about <u>The Seven Mysteries of Life</u>. Sez every puff of the air he takes now is a wonder. Here's the yarn.

According to Welcome's book the average breath you breathe contains about ten sextillion atoms, a number you can write as 10^{22}. And, as it turns out, the atmosphere of the earth contains just about the same number of breaths — ten sextillion. Running out the multiplication; 10^{22} atoms in each of 10^{22} breaths, means there are about 10^{44} atoms of air blowing around our planet. This means that every time you breathe you take in about one atom from all the breaths in the whole sky. Every time you exhale you send back about one atom to all the little breaths out there in our atmosphere.

"Now, here's the amazing part," sez Welcome: "About four billion of us do this twenty-thousand times a day. As a result each breath you breathe contains a quadrillion (10^{15}) atoms breathed by other folks within the past few weeks, and more than a million atoms breathed personally sometime by each and every person on earth."

Well, that led me and Welcome to pour a little libation for our ownselves. I mean, like Welcome sez, the thought of breathing a million atoms that had been in Madonna's body just last week can leave you just a little palpitated. One thing led to another and pretty soon I started telling my pal Welcome about some heavy duty breathing of my own. It's called Ki.

The Chinese have a name for the *living energy* in the universe, they call it "Ch'i". The Japanese call it "Ki". And in Japan there is a martial art called "Aikido", the path of non-dissention, which utilizes Ki principles. One of these principles is *relax completely*. When you are fully relaxed then your life energy or Ki can flow.

Now, relaxation and I aren't what you'd call best buddies. My heart attack in '76 and my by-pass surgery in '88 sorta put me in the Type A category. You know the kind — work 'til they drop; then do it again and sweat the details. I'd feel sorry for 'em except I am one. Which makes me take notice when someone pulls my coat to a way of relaxing.

Big-wigs in white coats have been interested in the health-giving qualities of relaxation techniques for years. Guy by the name of Benson at Harvard advocates deep breathing meditation daily for anyone at risk with heart problems. But even in these hectic days of stress and anxiety in a slow economy not many people it seems will dedicate 20 minutes a day to their own good health. Crazy, isn't it? But, it's understandable.

Ki breathing is tough because it's so easy. All you have to do is control your mind and breathe deeply. A snap, huh? But it took me about three years to get into a steady routine.

Every morning now I take twenty minutes or so to inhale and exhale deeply. Rule one is to sit anyway you like but, keep the lower back straight. Rule two is to give your mind something to do and gently insist that it do just that. I give my mind the task of extending Ki as I exhale slowly through my mouth while relaxing completely. I imagine myself lighting up like a light bulb with rays of energy extending infinitely in all directions. On the long, slow inhale (through the nose) I imagine that same energy entering my center or one-point. And I keep at it.

Sure, my mind wonders off. It's plum easy to think about chasing Maude or some such. But I just treat those thoughts like clouds. Let 'em drift right through my noggin, now back to business. Maude could probably outrun me anyway.

Give it a try but don't expect any wonder cure. The results are solid but they're subtle and it takes time.

Maybe when you're breathing you'll be sharing atoms with Mother Teresa! Be careful, though. Welcome Owsley is out there puffin' too. And your mother told you to never have any truck with the likes of him.

On Life Boats

That damned Welcome Owsley is always after me to get a bigger boat: "Bill," he bellows, "yer always paddlin like mad to get your little boat around to face life's next big wave. Get a bigger boat!"

And it's true. First it's the tax audit. Next it's worrying about that pain in the chest. And I'm always fretting about my kids and even my grand kids. You never know what wave is going to swamp your little boat. So it pays to paddle like mad and keep a wary eye on every wave on the great ocean of life.

"Bill, stop that damned bailing," sez Owsley, "You spend all yer time throwing water out of the half-swamped little boat of yours. Get a bigger boat!"

So naturally I had to come back at old Welcome with the question, "Just how in the hell do you expect me to get a bigger boat? You yourself are always everlastingly preaching in my ear that life ain't holdin a good hand but playin a poor one well."

"Exactly," sez Welcome: "To play a bad hand well you've gotta have a bigger boat. Then when those monster waves come surging through your life you can sit on the deck of your ocean liner and admire their speed and power." When life's storms are raging, you can calmly steer your great ship toward safer waters." "Strong Ki," sez Welcome, "that's your bigger boat."

So I asked Welcome about this Ki business. He said it's mostly training the unconscious. Training your "fighting mind" for one thing.

One exercise in Aikido involving fighting mind is called *unliftable body*. In this exercise two people lift under your arms, pick you up, and try to touch your head to the ceiling, more or less. And, more or less, everybody tends to think, "down; I must resist."

Their fighting mind takes over. When you do that it is sort of like pulling back with your arm when someone takes your hand and tries to pull you out of a deep, soft chair. If you think *pull back* you pop right up out of the chair. You give the other person power by your resistance.

So in the unliftable body exercise forget about *opponents* and *resistance*. Instead, think "up" — "You two people and I will lift; but we have to lift the whole dojo (training hall)."

When you get it right your body is unliftable. And it's funny as hell to watch Maude, who weighs about 125 pounds dripping wet, when a couple of big bruisers grab her under the arms and strain a gut trying to put air under her feet.

That Maude she just smiles sweetly and will not be moved. It's called getting a bigger boat.

Extending Calmness

Well now, if you've been a regular customer of these yarns, you'd know that Bill and Maude are Aikido students. So those of you that haven't done your homework, why just drift on back to the want ads. Buy a Nubian goat or something. Cause the regulars here are gonna relax and unlax, so to speak, Aikido style.

"Do", you know, means a "way" or a "path" in Japanese. "Ki" refers to breath or living energy. So Aikido is "the path of living energy, a path of non-dissention." You blend or flow with the force of another rather than trying to block or stop the energy of an attacker.

Calmness is a big part of the discipline of Aikido. Calmness is cumulative. That's right, cumulative. You can build it up in body and psyche just like a bank account. You can learn to "calm up" rather than merely calming down.

Extending calmness, extending Ki, is something you and I do just naturally off and on. Well, maybe a little more off than on. Aikido studies make you more aware of extending Ki all the time.

I remember my first born kid. Kristina. She was a bit fussy and cranky as a baby. Could ya blame her? She'd been born to a couple of greenhorns. But I soon developed this trick of putting Tina on my chest where she could feel my calmness. Then I'd put a little jiggle in my jog and walk her to sleep. Did it most nights. But one time I got home late from a P.T.A. meeting and Kristina's aunt plus my wife were there to meet me at the door. "Do something about this squalling kid," they chorused.

In jig time I had 'er asleep using my chest and jiggle routine. Looking back to what I was doing I now call it extending Ki naturally.

I remember also holding hands with Bobby, a little league pitcher I was coaching. Yep, just walked to the mound and held his hands to drain the scared out of him. Oh, I'd gab about this or that, nothing important because what I'd found out was that two minutes of holding hands calmed him right down so he could throw heat again for strikes.

Back I'd go to the dugout. And back to the dugout would go the batters, blown down by the high, hard heat of a calm pitcher. Looking back I'd call it extending Ki naturally.

The trick is to learn to extend Ki when the bases of life are loaded with opposition runners, nobody out, and you're behind in the count with a good hitter at the plate waving a big stick. Somehow it don't come natural. Extending calmness is mostly a learned and practiced path.

Becoming Accident Prone

Come on. Follow me. You and I are going to knock on death's door. This brazen activity is inspired by the book, <u>Living Fully, Dying Well</u>. The book consists of dialogues among a Rabbi, a Nun, and a Buddhist. They follow these dialogues with a section of exercises and reflections. Both the dialogues and the reflections grew out of about 10 years work in offering workshops and seminars on death and dying. The premise is that one can come to live more deeply, more intently, and more richly by knocking on death's door, that is, by confronting one's mortality directly. I've read the book and find the work compelling. One of their ideas I found immediately useful. It's an idea about spiritual growth. The Rabbi, almost as an aside during the dialogues, remarked that enlightenment is always an accident. You can't accumulate credits toward enlightenment nor can you make it a goal to strive toward. It either will happen or it won't. But, says the Rabbi, spiritual practice makes you more accident prone!

No, of course I'm not enlightened but I do engage in two spiritual practices. First, I go to church. Yeah, yeah, yeah; I know a lot of you believe that church is the last place you'd go to look for anything, most especially spirituality. But if there is one thing I've learned about me it's that I'm spiritually lazy when I'm not in community. I seek spiritual community within the church. That's one of my practices. The second is meditation. I've been meditating for a rather long time, mainly in conjunction with my past training in Aikido, a Japanese martial art that emphasizes "Ki" development, "Ki" being the life force extant in the universe. Aikido teaches a form of meditation involving Ki breathing. You sit "seiza" with your back very straight ("seiza" is sitting on your knees with your feet tucked straight back). My knees no longer permit the seiza position so I use a straight-back chair. First, you find your "one-point", your center of balance located deep in your lower belly. Then you take in a very long, very deep breath imagining you are drawing in Ki to your one-point. Importantly, the breath is drawn low into an expanding belly, not high and shallow in just the upper lungs. Then you start a long, slow exhale sounding "ha" which is said to be the mother sound of the Japanese language. You extend that exhale as long as you can even after you can no longer voice the "ha" sound. During the exhale you imagine your one—point lighting up like an incandescent bulb sending Ki into the universe in all directions. Then you inhale and exhale again. Normally I do that for about twenty minutes every morning at about six. It is a way of habituating myself to being in this world all day, every day as an emitter of strong plus Ki life energy. I said "normally" in the above sentence because for too many months now I have not been practicing Ki breathing . My all-too-normal state of spiritual laziness has taken over. Living Fully, Dying Well has been a useful kick in the behind reminding me that while I can't be programmatic in striving for enlightenment, I can consciously try to become accident prone. I can practice Ki breathing. Grace may or may not find me.

Stone and Steel

Questions

Material: found cast iron and stone, 27" height, 12" width, 6" depth
Owners: Nancy Haas, San Francisco, California

Questions

Hey gang, hurry to our place and see my new sculpture. It will only be here a few weeks, then it's off to its new home in San Francisco. Here's the yarn.

The sculpture involves questions both dark and bright, both regret and promise. Because, you see, the piece is all about the emotional turmoil involved in divorce. Years ago, my first wife left me and a few months later sued for divorce. I embarked on a three-Valium weekend, followed by other assorted emotional adventures.

Later, I signed up for a Beginning Experience weekend up in Seattle. It's a weekend put on by folks who have lost a spouse, either to death or divorce, for others in the same fix. The weekend is modeled after the five stages of grief proposed by Kubla Ross in her book <u>Death and Dying</u>. The grief stages are denial, bargaining, anger, depression and acceptance.

The structure for the Beginning Experience weekend shapes up like this. After a few preliminaries, two quite ordinary people read their very personal statements about the actuality of the denial stage of grieving in their lives. No advice given. No generalization about sexist men or bitchy women. No highfalutin ideas about relationship, it is simply a straight-out look at denial in a real life. The two stories sandpaper your psyche and march you off to a private space where you can talk to yourself and write in your journal about the role denial might play in your own grieving. After which you find yourself in a room with 4 to 6 other souls spending an hour sharing as much as you feel comfortable with. The rules are two. First: "Stay in the room," that is, talk only about you own feelings. Second: "Don't try to fix anybody," just listen.

After the small group sharing, the big group gets back together for round two — bargaining. Then on through each of the stages.

The weekend leads you into examining the dark, somber questions in your present circumstance as well as the bright, promising question facing you too. You end up writing a letter closing the door gently on the past.

All this remembered emoting came back to mind because the woman asking me to carve a stone for her was herself in the throes of a divorce. And that fact caused me to take those remembered feelings with me over to the stone emporium, Pacific Stonescape on Highway 34 outside Corvallis. I ruminated among them boulders off and on for several weeks but nothing clicked. So I took my little self down to Schnizer Steel, in Eugene, where my eyeballs glommed onto a huge, probably 40 or 50 pound steel hook. Voila! Turn that bad boy downside up and it becomes a 50 pound cast steel question mark.

The sculpture ended up being four steel hooks (or question marks), a large one painted fire engine red and three small ones painted glossy black. I mounted those babies on an appropriate stone and added a red glass ball. Called the whole mess, "One Period, Four Question Marks."

Like I say, it will only be here for a short while. So hurry on out if you just can't wait to see four painted steel question marks mounted on a rock with a red ball thrown in. Most people visiting the piece just slowly shake their heads, get back in their rigs, and zoom away to the normal world, where people grieve privately, silently, and corrosively.

Getting Stoned

During summers in my high school days I worked for the P.L. Lumber Company on the survey crew. We laid out truck roads, surveyed property lines, ran chopping lines and even did a little timber cruising. Pat Doyle, our Irish boss, would look at us stumbling, bumbling adolescents and mumble under his breath, "Main strength and awkwardness!" And it was true enough 'cept bein skinny and adenoidal we weren't all that strong.

But main strength and awkwardness is still my way, especially when Maude and I get all heated up about building a garden Japanese style. Only Maude, you see, is the engineer of the outfit. Oregon Bill supplies the other two ingredients for heaving boulders — main strength and awkwardness.

Only three things are really necessary for a Japanese garden — water, rocks, and evergreen trees. Today, ponder, we're talkin rocks of the boulder kind.

First, in the rock biz, are the little fellers of 200 pounds or so. Then there are the big bruisers up to a couple of tons or more. Puny rocks just don't belong in a Japanese garden. A certain "presence" is required.

Maude and I took three years to gather the boulders for our garden. Stashed 'em all around the parking lot and gave them names like "Voluptuous" and "Behemoth".

Got some of our boulders down at Bond Butte south of here out by Lake Creek Grange. Got others up the Calapooia River. But the best deal in used rocks was up at Morse Bros., Inc. in Sweet Home. They'd load boulders for you off their gravel quarry for a dollar a ton, you haul 'em.

Back in '83 Morse Bros., Inc. didn't have much call for boulders. Just rolled em out of the way while they scratched out the sand and gravel. After they got down in the pit a ways they had boulders all over the place, a regular boulder emporium you might call it. All you had to do was walk around the store looking for boulders that spoke to you. Across the boulder emporium would roar a big-jawed front-end loader to pick up your stone and delicately place it on your low-boy trailer. Off you'd go.

Morse Bros., Inc. equipment was really handy because in those days Maude and I were getting our boulders using the latest technology available when they were building those pyramids in Egypt back in 4000 BC — the lever, the inclined plane, and 2000 slaves. Only, Maude had me and my come-a-long instead of 2000 slaves. Like I say, it's a main strength and awkwardness show getting those boulders out of the quarry, on to the truck, out of the truck, over to the garden, then positioned just right so their best face shows. Every boulder has a face doncha know.

Maude calls the shots. I do the huff and puff.

One time up on the Calapooia River during low water in August we pulled up on the river bar where another couple were running a little two-bit gold dredging show. Mr., he was busy as hell mucking around in the river turning over stones looking for an ore bearing layer of gravel. Mrs., she was lolly gagging under the shade of a tree, knitting or reading, or something like that.

We busted out on that river bar and I commenced getting out our fancy equipment — iron crowbar, chains, come-along, and so forth. I set to molesting a humongous boulder Maude and I had been eyeing for sometime. Just as I got good and involved in my grunting and cussing, why Mrs. Gold Miner Widow Lady she sidles up to Maude and asks what's going on. Maude explained politely why I was panting and heaving so , but she could tell Mrs. Gold Widow was mighty skeptical. So Maude backed off a little and started to explain about Japanese gardens. Just then Mrs. Gold Widow patted Maude on the arm and said, "Lady, I thought MY husband was crazy!"

Happened right there on the upper Calapooia. Summer of '84.

Stoned Again

We're talkin garden boulders here one more time. Now stop rattling that paper that-a-ways. With just five minutes of reading here you'll amaze your neighbors with how much you know about stones in a Japanese garden. Why, you never know when over to the Grange Hall, or, after church someone is apt to quiz you about the "wa" of your garden stones.

Everybody's gotta have wa! So listen up!

First off, know that every stone has a face, a direction it must look toward. Japanese folk are big about knowing the faces of stones. Additionally, they believe the art of the garden is getting your ego out of the way so that the stone can be its own true self.

They tell the story in Japan of a rich Westerner being introduced to a very, very old Buddhist garden. Sure enough, the rich Westerner just had to have a certain stone from that garden to take back home. So she asked to buy the stone and received a politely ambiguous reply. She asked again. And again her request was not quite replied to directly. Finally she demanded to buy the stone and named a very large sum. This time the Monk answered saying: "You must understand, Madam, our temple searched for thirty years for this stone. When we found it we studied its face for ten years. Two thirds of the stone you see is buried underground. So you see, it can't be sold."

Stones, doncha know, are the *bones* of a Japanese garden, the skeleton so to speak. That is why in ancient Japan master gardeners could often be heard humming softly, "Oh, the foot stone connected to the leg stone. Now hear the wa of the ..." All in Japanese, of course.

Water and evergreen trees are *flesh* to cover the bones of the garden. Your job as a gardener is to quiet yourself sufficiently so that it is the garden that speaks rather than your ego. I don't know just exactly what that means but it sounds exotic as hell don't it?

I do try to study the faces of my stones. When you get the knack it's funny as hell to drive around Eugene and spot yards where the stones turn their backs, look up in the sky, or stand on their heads. I recommend that you don't reveal this to too many people because a lotta folk are apt to just flat out tell ya you ought to up and move down there, hug trees, picket the president, and all like that there.

But I can tell you how to turn boulders into cash, moola, the long green and lots of it. Happened when I was visiting a sculptor just this side of the Golden Gate and out on the coast. This bird specialized in monumental stone and redwood stump pieces you might set up in corporate headquarters or up in the board room of Big Bucks, Inc.

Visiting his place I oohed and aahed at the redwood stumps littering the landscape until my eyes glommed onto a large green serpentine stone all river-washed so it looked slicker 'n snot. It was love at first sight. I had to have the stone. Then he told me the price — $15,000. "And," said he, "it would fetch $125,000 in Japan."

So, knowing I couldn't buy the stone I began to get sly, quizzing him on where it was from. Believing the chances were one in a zillion this hick from Oregon would know anything about anything, he said, "Oh, up on the Van Duzen in Northern California."

"Oh," sez I, "where on the Van Duzen?"

"Humm," sez he, "have you ever heard of Bridgeville?"

Well, now, have I ever heard of Bridgeville!?! Turns out Bridgeville is the first stop out the Van Duzen River to my great grandfather Cobb's hotel out past Low Gap but not so far as the Devil's Back Bone or South Fork Mountain. It's on the road my Uncle Cletus hit that night he was twelve and his sisters told him they wouldn't fix his supper until he filled the woodbox. So Cletus he got his dander up and lit out to ride the 40 mountain miles to Grandpa Cobb's ranch on his bicycle. He'd show his sisters how to treat a working man.

Next August when the river is low you'll find me on the Van Duzen about 300 yards downriver from the Bridgeville store. The first $125,000 rock is mine. Help yer own self to all the rest.

I still don't know a damned thing about wa, 'cept a body's gotta have it.

Listens to the Stone

Awlright folks, enough of the light and fluffy. Oregon Bill is going for the BIG THINK.

Stand back and give the Dude room to roll out the four-bit words. I mean we're talkin something on the order of chaos theory here or maybe even fuzzy logic.

So, everybody now, on the count of three, screw your eyebrows together and remember Mr. Hardwick back in the fifth grade. Remember when Welcome Owsley asked him why you inverted and multiplied when dividing a fraction? Old Hardwick got all red and his eyes bugged out filling the board with those denominators, numerators, reciprocals and such. It was ponderous stuff.

Got the picture? OK. Hang on and we'll spin out the whole yarn. It all begins with the idea of entropy and a visit to see the works of my hero, Isamu Noguchi.

First of all, haul out the old Funk and Wagnel's like I did and look up the word "entropy". Either Mr. Funk or Mr. Wagnel, I don't know which one it was, though I suspect it was probably their wives down in the dictionary-works unraveling words the boys had gotten all screwed up because of their all-fired arguments about chaos theory or fuzzy logic. Anyways, F & W defines entropy as "the degradation of matter and energy in the universe to an ultimate state of inert uniformity."

Sort of reminds you of one of those teenagers hangin by the bench up town, don't it? Or, my place up on Hwy 228 — the whole outfit is long on inert not to mention degradation-of-matter.

Now, here's the grabber. It's easy to get into your noggin the idea that our lives are entropic. Sure seems like it's a long slide downhill to "an ultimate state of inert uniformity." I mean old age looks like entropy city to me. Talk about your run down, your inert.

Come on, fess up, that's what's in your noggin isn't it?

But it ain't necessarily so. Life don't have to be entropic. Take my main man Noguchi, for example. He's a stone man, of course. A sculptor.

Isamu Noguchi was born to an American mother and a Japanese father prior to WWII. After an apprenticeship with Brancusi in Paris, Noguchi struck out on his own as a sculptor. Early on he began a twenty-year friendship with Martha Graham designing sets for her dance troupe. Went on to design parks and playgrounds in Israel and elsewhere. Did the garden for the Unesco headquarters in Paris. Designed the Peace Park bridge in Hiroshima. Mounted a stone and acari (a kind of Japanese lantern) show in Japan.

The old gentleman died at age 84 working on his tsukabai series. A tsukabai is the stone garden basin where you wash your hands, thus purifying yourself, prior to the Japanese tea ceremony. Noguchi's interpretation was to take about a five foot high piece of columnar basalt and cut off a flat top. He'd carve a small bowl in that top then polish that surface plus one or two others. He'd drill a hole in the basin down through the stone, then balance the upright column so perfectly that the water would rise continuously in the bowl and spread a thin film out evenly across the top and down all sides into a collecting pan hidden by a layer of smooth small granite stones.

One of the tsukabai is set in Noguchi's sculpture garden and retrospective show at his former studio in The Queens, New York. As you walk among Noguchi's stone works, arranged by decades, you become aware that here is a life that gathered force, gathered clarity to the very last day. This man grew in power and simplicity in every decade. When asked his secret, Noguchi replied, "I listen to the stone."

On Cutting Away the Excess

When Oregon Bill grows up he wants to become a sculptor. It's easy you know. Michaelangelo himself said it was a snap. All you had to do was imagine the form in the stone and then cut away the excess.

Cinch, huh?

Actually old Bill has tried and tried to pound on stone to sculpt a form or two. The results have been — how did the instructor phrase it? — oh yes, "interesting".

Here's the yarn.

Matt, one of my long-ago instructors (I've been chasing this sculpture fantasy for years) specialized in one-liners. He'd lurk around, pacing impatiently at the edge of the class just waiting for you to ask for comments. This one piece I had was a block of sandstone about four feet high, eighteen inches wide, and twelve inches deep. I'd been pecking on it for three or four sessions rounding the back (it stood upright on the four foot axis) and hollowing a curve on the front. On this recessed curve I had started the profile of a face in low relief.

Eventually, I called on Matt to make some words over my stone. He swooped down grinning like mad at the chance to announce loudly his verdict: "Well, Bill, it's obviously a terrific urinal!" The rest of the class laughed wildly, of course, as Matt fumbled with his fly. "But then," and here he put his foot up and shoved the stone over and as it lay rocking gently on the floor, said, "it could just as well be a bird bath!"

The second line killed 'em. I mean everybody busted a gut laughing. But, come to think of it, they were great one-liners. And not too far off the mark.

I mean you've got to have a strong ego to sculpt. Your work

is so *there*. It's so damned three dimensional. And no matter what pretty words you float on the air, it doesn't change the stone, the wood, the bronze, or the whatever, not one bit.

I got taught this strong ego message after my first heart attack some years ago. Figuring the universe was telling me I better get serious about the dream of becoming a sculptor, I signed up for a bronze casting class at the university. About four weeks into the course, the instructor announced that we needed to have five forms in wax next week. Then we'd have a public critique of our work.

You should have heard the sphincters on those twenty-year-olds snap shut.

Only half the class showed up on the day of the critique. The rest had dropped the course. One guy who did come wore a huge overcoat and sort of held his waxes in close behind the coat so no one could see them. Another guy stood right next to a big post in that basement room so about half the class had their view blocked. One gal brought her waxes in a brown paper bag and wouldn't even take 'em out.

After the critique another quarter of the class dropped. I realized then how tender is the nineteen-year-olds' ego. And how private is most college work — only you and the professor ever see it, The better to cushion fragile egos.

But by that time I had been kicked around a little by life and was pushing fifty. Besides, I had studied with Fast Eddie.

Fast Eddie sold pornographic sculpture in Los Angeles. Genitalia, wouldn't you know, cast in polished bronze. And he had a terrific come-on for middle class, middle age types who signed up for his adult education courses. He hired a nekkid model.

So there she was in the buff. And there we were all flushed and fumbling with our wax trying to capture an impression without drooling on the floor. I mean we were middle-aged, middle-class, middle-brained, middle-everything.

The model was classy though. She even conducted her own

critiques (Fast Eddie was off doing something phallic or vaginal). She'd get down off the dais, come around and use her bod up close and personal to comment on how you were doing.

It's really un-nerving, you know, to have a very young lady sidle over to you, grab her ownself and say, "It looks like this, dummy. You blind, or what?"

The tag line to this yarn is just as goofy. The next day I saw this very same young lady walking down the hall at the place where I work. So now when the sculpture class rolls around, I sit there and remember how terrific she looks fully clothed.

"Just imagine the form in the stone and…"

Hey, I think I'm getting the hang of it.

Artist to Artist

The faithful reader of this column knows that Oregon Bill is going to be a sculptor when he grows up. The faithless reader of this column knows that the old goat just turned eighty. The chances of him growing up let alone becoming a sculptor, those chances are, like, slim or none.

But, wouldn't you know, while slurping a mug of joe down at Randy's Main Street Coffee, Birthday Bill met up with an old art teacher of his, a feller by the name of Brown, Clint Brown. He teaches, Brown does, over to the Agriculture and Mechanics College in Corvallis. Back in '76, after his first heart attack, Bill took a couple of classes from Professor Clint.

Down at Randy's they slapped each other on the back, they did, and then went through the standard ritual. Ran through all the clap-trap old gaffers use when they meet up with someone they haven't seen for a spell and don't hardly remember:

…"Been a long time;"

…"My yer looking good;"

…"Whatever happened to what's his face?"

Then, Brown, right out of the blue, he up and announces he's just published a book and he's gonna give our boy Bill a copy. That book is called <u>Artist to Artist</u> it's a compilation of inspiration and advice created when them graphic types stop making art and start making words over their art.

Well, "Ol Bill, he got the book, took a gander at it, and has a few tidbits to share. He was interested, of course, in the quotes from his personal heroines and heroes. Folks like Louise Nevelson, Dame Barbara Hepworth, Sir Henry Moore, Isamu Noguchi (actually, Noguchi didn't make the cut), Auguste Rodin, and all like that there.

First quote was a lulu; inspirational you might say. My man

Rodin, back before WWI, he hauls off and sez, "Sculpture is quite simply the art of depression and protuberance."

Easy for him to say!

Bronze cat he was, that Rodin, so he was all the time working in clay pushing it up here, gouging it out there — protoobing and depressing right regular. Made cast impressions of his finished clay. Poured in a little molten bronze and, voila, knocked off for lunch — another masterpiece whomped up.

A second quote, one from Sir Henry Moore, brought me back down to earth. Moore is an English bloke, you know, that punched holes in his sculpture. "Negative space" he called it. Well, Moore he up and opines, "What makes good sculptor is a good mind."

Now Maude often describes Bill's mind in colorful terms but "good" ain't one of 'em. Very sobering those words of Maude and Moore.

To make matters worse, Louise Nevelson, she of the wonderfully intricate walls of patterned black wooden pieces, she says it ain't good enough just to think well about form. The thinking has to be swift. Imagination of "flash thinking" is where it's at, sez Nevelson.

Flash Nevelson goes on to talk about her work habits. "I get up at six in the morning. And I wear cotton clothes so that I can sleep in them or I can work in them — I don't want to waste time… sometimes I could work two or three days and not sleep."

Well, I don't want to brag or nuthin but the regulars down at Randy's know I been doin that for years. Why just last week folks had a grand time naming the projects I was working on by looking at the duds I was wearing. Little dab of grease here, some sawdust there, stains on the hands, shoes untied, paint in the hair — they all told a story of art on the make. It's just the two or three days work without sleep — that's the part I don't have down.

But, all said: "I'm gonna stick with my main man Rodin — depression and protuberance. Yes sir, when this cold fog lifts and the warm Oregon rains return, I'm gonna take my little self out to my studio and poosh 'em up, gouge 'em out like there ain't no tomorrow. Come on down. We'll have a cuppa joe and make words over the forms, artist to artist.

Cosmic Joke

Queen's Bishop

Material: found cast iron, 42" height, 14" width, 14" depth
Owner: Garvin and Betty Jabusch, California

Spiritual Greed

Been harvesting hazelnuts out on my place this week. Boy, has it been a dry year! The orchard floor is a crazy quilt of big cracks. Didn't harvest a nut this year actually. They all rolled down the cracks in the earth!

Harvesting hazelnuts is an interesting exercise in greed you know. Tells you how greedy you are every year. Yep, first nut drops early in September but the last nut won't fall until December. Meanwhile, the Oregon monsoons are liable to begin any week which always shuts down the harvest. My cheap, raggedy equipment won't work in a heavy morning dew, let alone a full scale early fall rainstorm. So the big question every year is when to start harvesting. Do you get after it now or let a few more nuts fall? Like I say, the whole process is a kind of greed index for farmer Bill from year to year.

Speaking of greed always reminds me of my pal Welcome Owsley's story about being a Sufi. Yeah, old Welcome up and hauled off a while back and decided to become a full fledged Sufi. No, he didn't become one of those whirling dervishes seeking spiritual ecstasy by spinning around faster and faster in a mad dance. Instead, he thought he'd become a wise fool like Nasrudin.

The Sufi Nasrudin is famous for his teaching stories, usually about a fool. You see one of those stories about every two years or so on television. I think I first saw "the light is better here" story in the fifties when Red Skelton did it. There was Red down on his hands and knees under a street lamp doing his famous drunk routine. Along comes the straight man who asks Red what he's looking for. Red tells him he's lost his watch. The two of them grope around for a few minutes on their hands and knees until the straight man in exasperation asks Red just where he lost the fool watch. Red points to the dark alley and says, "Over there."

"Then why are you looking out here?" asks the foil.

"Because," says Red, "the light is a whole lot better out here!"

Like I say, Nasrudin is one of Welcome's role models.

So, Welcome, he's studying like mad to become a Sufi. Met with his spiritual teacher damn near every week. Took out after each spiritual exercise his teacher could suggest. I mean, in looking back, Ol' Welcome says he was seeing people's auras and everything.

Then one day he up and quits his Sufi studies cold turkey.

Down at the tavern one Saturday night I jumped Welcome about his back-sliding ways. Ol' Welcome, he just looks me in the eye and says, "Bill, spiritual greed is still greed!"

We looked at our long neck beers for quite awhile. Then we shot some pool and called it a night.

On Snapping Sphincters

That fool Owsley is at it again. I caught him telling Sufi stories over a couple of espressos uptown at Randy's Main Street Coffee last week. He had the good patrons there mighty riled up over his plans to get rich exporting canned goods to China and the Philippines. I arrived just as Welcome was high-tailing it out the back door. After the growling died down I pieced together what had happened. Here 'tis.

Seems like one of the regulars had come in for coffee tying his pooch by its leash on that little tree the city planted next to the sidewalk out the front door. The dog greeted each morning coffee club member with a madly wagging tail. That exuberant canine greeting behavior led to a round of "ain't-they-cute" dog stories while sipping regular Joe or espresso, depending on your caffeine persuasion.

Well, Ol' Welcome, he busts in out of the rain, bellys up to the bar and orders a double espresso just like he belonged indoors with civilized people. But folks said afterwards he had a sort of cockeyed gleam in his eye right from the get-go. At any rate, the regulars all agreed Welcome listens to the dog stories for a few minutes and then stops slurping his espresso long enough to chime in with a remark coming way out of left field: "Astoria," he sez, "has fish canneries you can buy for a song." "Yessir," he goes on, "fishing has gone to pot and a Brownsville entrepreneur such as myself could start hisself a nice canning business up there in Astoria. Just need a little working capital."

The cute dog story crowd looked at each other, shrugged and went back to admiring man's best friend which at the time definitely wasn't Welcome Owsley.

Ol' Welcome, though, couldn't be headed off and followed up his Astoria cannery observations with a few facts about Oregon dog pounds. "When you add 'em up," sez Welcome, "they put to sleep about 200 dogs a day in Oregon."

The last remark brought the cute-dog-story crowd up short. Welcome said afterwards you could hear sphincters snap shut right and left.

And Ol' Welcome, he moved in for the clincher: "Yep," he continued, "some places in China as well as in the Philippines folks love dog meat. What I figure on doing is going up to Astoria, canning that wasted SPCA dog meat and exporting it. Rin Tin Tin in a tin, you might say. Oughta make a dent in that there balance of trade problem we got."

Slapped three dollars on the bar and high tailed it out the back door, Welcome did.

I caught up with Owsley a day or two later down at the tavern and asked him what the dickens that canned dog meat foolishness was all about: "Just doin' a Nasrudin Number," says Welcome, "helping folks expand their awareness." Well, I've hung around Owsley long enough to know about Nasrudin the Sufi mystic. Hung out in the Middle East, Nasrudin did, a spell ago. He was famous for his wise fool stories that caused folks back then to scratch their heads at the perverse logic of the punch line to those stories. My pal Owsley claims he's a little league Nasrudin himself. Take his fishing number for example.

Owlsey loves to catch a fishing crowd swapping yarns then he'll bust in telling about casting a pork chop on a hook up Kirk Avenue and reeling in a thirty pound pooch right up to the porch.

Sphincters snap shut in that crowd too!

You Oughta Be in the Comics

Probably you all have been the butt of a joke somewhere along the line. Happens to the best of folks, even Oregon Bill. Turns out that Bill was once a cosmic joke. The whole universe sorta sniggered and chortled to behold his comical condition. Here's the yarn.

Seems like Bill was back in Arkansas visiting his cousin when his wife of twenty-seven years got in the car and drove off. Not that this was a surprise to anyone. Bill and his wife had worked hard at the marriage but they could just never get it together enough to keep it together. And so she vamoosed.

It was Christmas time and my cousin and her husband were bound for Florida to visit relatives there. So I was left alone in my cousin's house waiting to catch an early flight the next day for New York and then to England where my wife and I had rented an apartment for three months in Wimbledon outside London.

About two in the morning the telephone rings and it's a heavy breather. Now, a body doesn't handle too many calls like that and after a few lusty pants I hung up the phone figuring the guy is after my cousin. I'm just an accident that happened to happen.

Then the phone rings again. It's the heavy breather one more time.

This time he has a few raspy suggestions and the light finally dawns. Hey, it's my body that's involved here.

Turns out it's the guy next door and he's rasping nervously these nimble suggestions because his wife and infant son are asleep in the next room. Turns out too, all three families had just attended a Moravian Love Fest two days before. A Moravian Love Fest is a church celebration breaking bread and singing carols in Christian fellowship.

Some fellowship he had in mind.

I put down the telephone, found a baseball bat, locked the bedroom door, and stayed up all night just like any calm, confirmed and practicing heterosexual would do.

But I knew right then the gods were funnin' me. Why else would a homosexual advance come my way within hours of the breakup of a twenty-seven year marriage?

There was more to come.

I climbed on the plane to New York that morning, flew on to London and ended up catching a local train the short way South to Wimbledon where sight unseen we had rented an apartment.

It was late at night when I arrived and as the taxi turned the corner to the apartment, there at the end of the street in two foot high orange neon letters was the name of my old home town in Northern California... *Fortuna*. It turned out to be a Chinese delicatessen.

As a youngster I had lived in Fortuna, California and had graduated from high school there. Now, here was my home town spelled out in neon letters two feet high, on the street where I was going to live for the next three months in Wimbledon, England. It was a gas.

So I walked up to the door of the house we had rented and tried the key only to find it was locked from the inside. After a lot of banging and shouting I found the place was already taken by a rich New York teenage snot on her way back to New York from Greece.

She decided to stay over in Wimbledon a few more days and wasn't going to let me in!? I mean this kid had a black belt in assertiveness training. I'm paying for the place, have the key, and *she's* not going to let *me* in!

So I bust in. She runs screaming bloody murder upstairs and locks the door to the only bedroom and bathroom! I fall asleep on the couch.

I mean when you're a cosmic joke you just have to grin, look the gods right in the eye, and try not to flinch.

But my luck changed.

The Black Belt kid had a horrible complexion and used to stand for hours at the kitchen sink using special ointments and stuff to make that red, pimply face presentable. My break came when I accidentally (Freud has a few ideas about "accidents") left a fresh S.O.S. pad in one of her make-up dishes at the kitchen sink. An S.O.S. pad you know is a kind of steel wool pad with some sort of junk in it you use to scrub pots and pans, and bathroom sinks.

All I know is that about make-up time the next morning Black Belt ran screaming like a banshee out of the kitchen, up the stairs, then out the front door and I never seen her again. I figured she tried the S.O.S. pad as a complexion aid.

But, all told, being a cosmic joke does frazzle the nerves.

Cracks a Funny

Annie Dillard writes in her book "Pilgrim at Tinker Creek": "The question of agnosticism is, Who turned on the lights? The question from faith is, Whatever for?" Well now, I was given a partial answer to the second question just last Monday. It's because the great power in this universe, believe it or not, gets bored by eternity and finds amusement in pointing out how absurd our tawdry little lives can sometimes be. Monday night I was the punch line in a cosmic joke over at the ER at Lebanon Hospital. Here's the yarn.

Actually, it started on Sunday, when I phoned my daughter in Minneapolis. As we talked along, I inquired when my grandson Daniel was going to get himself married and sire a great grandchild for his decrepit and aging grandfather, who is me. Kristina replied blithely, "Oh Dad, Daniel says it will be at least ten years!" To which I replied, "Tell Daniel that if he waits ten years, great-grandbaby and great-grandpa will both be wearing diapers!"

I had cracked a funny and Kristina giggled appreciatively. But normally I'm not a quick wit at all, so I went around all that Sunday just full of myself and my line..." great-grandbaby and great-grandpa will both be wearing diapers". I had cracked a funny...*heeheeheeeheee.*

Got up at 3 a.m. Monday morning when Doc and Ed picked me up to go fishing. Doc had arranged a guide to go after the spring Chinook on the Columbia River, a primo fish and primo fishing experience.

Jumped in the car, I did, with the boys and set off for Linnton just down river from Portland. Stopped at a rest stop on the way with an aching tummy, but I couldn't make any water. Didn't think much of it until we got to the boat landing, met the guide, and I slipped over to the facilities for another try. No luck. The tummy-ache a little more insistent.

Into the boat we all climbed and ran out to Davis Bar where we trolled down the Columbia for about two miles or so then ran back up to run our herring once again just off the bottom in water 20 to 30 feet deep. Hooked three of them springers we did and landed two of them. Beautiful fish! But I'd been in growing pain all day, a pain now starting to localize on the left side. Passed no water.

At 3:30 p.m. we called it a successful day and ran back to the landing where I gave it another try. Still no luck.

Tried again at the South Santiam rest stop on the I-5 above Albany. By now I'm in a world of hurt, but I figure if I could just make it home, a little heat on the old belly would relax things and I'd be hunky-dory.

Staggered in the house, grabbed a heating pad, and insisted that Maude go ahead with her plans for Corvallis that evening. "I'll be fine," I told her. " A little heat on the belly and I'll be fine."

So I kicked the reluctant Maude out of the house. Not more than 15 minutes later I was sweating like a horse and hung over, I was, over the commode with the dry heaves. Luckily our neighbors Keren and Alan were home and together we made like the Indy 500 over to the Lebanon Hospital where they hustled me right in for a CAT scan, pain pills, and a catheter into the bladder.

The possibilities are two — either a kidney stone (not likely) or an enlarged prostate (quite likely). I'll find out Saturday. Meanwhile, while I'm not wearing diapers (yet), I do have a bag strapped to my leg which I empty every couple of hours. And every time I empty it, I swear, I hear a soft little chuckle and the words, "You cracked a funny, Oregon Bill."

Remembering Marie

Well now, I don't know why the memory came back. But it did. Brought back those old feelings of being a cosmic joke. Like in vaudeville days when the main man in the show, the lead comic, he was called the *Top Banana*. Seems like the main man in this universe, the *Top Banana*, so to speak, gets bored now and then and whomps up a small joke on me just for the giggle of it. Take for example that time, about 1959 it was , at the Convent in San Rafael (or was it Petaluma?).

I was married then and we had four kids and were living in a Quonset hut at Stanford Village, a WWII hospital in Menlo Park, on $3000 a year plus what I could make working at Bekins Van and Storage on weekends. I was a graduate student at Stanford, you see, and my brother-in-law worked at Bekins in Palo Alto. At the time Bekins was moving tons of offices out of San Francisco where corporations, like insurance businesses and such, were trying to move out of The City and down the peninsula toward San Jose where office space was cheaper. So, because I had an in at Bekins I got the big wages, $3.50 an hour, packing file cabinets up two flights of stairs — four-drawer cabinets fully loaded. They weighed a ton. It took two of us and a hand-truck, one of us on the handles of the hand-truck backing up the stairs, and one on the bottom doing the heavy lifting. At this particular second floor operation at Stanford Shopping Center my partner, the Neanderthal, said, "To hell with this," (he meant the bumping up of the heavy file cabinets one step at a time), and he lifted the whole she-bang, hand-truck and all, pushing me up two flights of stairs to the second floor. Spent the rest of the weekend, I did, trying to match the Neanderthal testosterone for testosterone.

But back to Marie and to me, the cosmic joke.

These were the days of the California Council on Teacher Education, which met yearly, so representatives from the state colleges could get together and compare notes on how they each manufactured teachers for the public schools. Stanford being too proud to mix with the hoi-pulloi of the state colleges but too crafty to risk being left out of anything, chose to send me to that year's conference in San Rafael (or was it Petaluma?). I was still a bushy-tailed graduate student though that year I had received an appointment as an acting instructor to cover for a regular professor on loan to Japan.

But to set this joke up proper you've got to remember that I was raised in Humboldt County in Northern California where loggers still told lusty tales of, "Taking our axes and running them 'Chinks' into Humboldt Bay". And it was historically accurate. In the 1870s thereabout there had been a Tong War in Eureka and the Caucasian mayor walked down the middle of the street between those two factions in the Chinese community and had been shot. A riot ensued in which white vigilantes pretty well destroyed the Chinese community with the Coast Guard transporting the survivors to San Francisco.

Yes, California has a long, tumultuous, and bitter history of racial conflict. And Oregon Bill is a third-generation Californian.

So I walk up to the registration desk there at the Convent in San Rafael (or was it Petaluma?) and identify myself by name. Immediately there is a great rustling of black robes among the Dominican sisters behind the registration counter. Standing there too is a very regal, very beautiful woman — an African American professor, and director of an internship teacher education program at the University of California, Berkeley. Her name is Mrs. Marie Fielder.

Mrs. Fielder turns, places her hand on the cheek of the pip-squeak graduate student from Stanford, who is me, and says: "My dear, I want you to be the first to know — I filed for divorce this very afternoon." Then she picks up *our* key and marches resolutely down the hall to her room. Only then did the Sisters explain to me there had been a mix up and a wrong assumption had been made when Mr. and Mrs. Fielder had sent in separate registrations for the conference.

Cross my heart, I heard a giggle in the heavens.

Falling Stars

Well now, Twelfth Night has come and gone reminding us all of the star over Bethlehem, the birth, and the three Wise men skulking back home by a different route to avoid reporting to Herod. This year, I thought about the possibility of not seeing that Star, or seeing but not believing the night sky over Bethlehem had I lived in that city that night long ago.

Surely some folks in that little hamlet were in their cups that night and took no note of the sky overhead. Could I have been in that tavern? Someone must have been shoveling animal dung in a stable and not looked up from the task. Was that me? Someone must have failed to look up into the heavens that night, so preoccupied they were about the rent money, about a son out galavanting who-knows-where, about a daughter making eyes at that no-good young Welcome Owsley kid who lived just down the street. All of which brings to mind the portents, the signs I fail to see in my life lived right now.

And what about you, dear reader?

I'll help you jump into this reverie by sharing a missing star-sign or two in my life. The first one is rather trivial, but it taught me a big lesson about my one-track mind. The other examples I'll share are a bit more haunting.

Time was, my wife up and left our marriage and I was in a lot of pain (as you can well imagine). Took off, she did, in the family car for New Orleans. We had been on our way to an apartment we'd rented for a month or so outside London. While visiting in the Mid-west the lady skedaddled. I flew on to London alone.

That was the end of a 27-year marriage. I coped with the pain by ritualizing my day: awoke, went running, breakfasted, worked five or six hours writing, caught a train for central London, visited the Tate Art Museum, bought a "New York Times" newspaper and read it over a pint, caught the train back to Wimbledon, prepared supper, read a short story or two (Isaac Bashevis Singer), then off to bed. I was a robot.

Then one day, a guy my age fell in step with me and inquired about the Tate Art Museum, and I took him in tow. Turns out he was a gamekeeper in a park in the north. So I kidded him about getting lost in his own capitol city and being rescued by a cheeky American. So he suggested we drop into a pub, have a pint, and he'd tell me how fast he could lose me in his game park. But I'm a robot — Times newspaper, train, supper, Singer, and then bed — so I declined and we parted. A block or two later I woke up. *"You missed a star, you dope!"* Ran back, but no gamekeeper. Had I accepted his invitation, we would have knocked back a pint or two, fell to telling lies about buck hunting, shooting pheasants, hunting dogs we had known, and the like, and he'd have left inviting me to his game park. But robotized me blacked out that small star right there in front of my nose.

The second star was one of pure ignorance and far more haunting. At age 45 or so, my mother revealed for the first time an event that took place back when I was 17 and bound for San Jose State to major in Elementary Education. My mother's story told of how she and my dad were formally called upon by Dr. and Mrs. Harold Comfort with a proposal: if I would become a Methodist minister, Helen and Harold Comfort would pay for my college education and then seminary school. Dad and Mom respectfully declined and never said a word about it until 30 years later.

Just three years after the invitation by Dr. and Mrs. Comfort, my father was crushed to death by a falling redwood tree. In anger at God, I left the church. It took me 30 years to find my way back. It was my marriage to the Maude girl that called me back into the fold.

Where are the signs of a greater power in the life you live? Twelfth Night asks that question.

A Little Epiphany

January sixth is called Twelfth Night because that is when we commemorate the Wise men coming into the presence of The Christ, the infant Jesus. Celebrating that event invites you and me to participate in that historic epiphany by regarding our everyday world in a new light, a sacred light. I had that experience recently. Here is what I make of it.

I have a son who is learning disabled in ways we have never fully understood. That disabling condition put him in special education classes throughout his school years. While he is the most philosophic thinker of all my children he still reads and writes at a level that is handicapping. He went back 16 times, for example, before he passed the written part of the drivers' license examination. Most of his work-life has been at the minimum wage level — washing dishes, washing cars, and so on.

Last fall my son rolled the dice yet again borrowing money on a credit card to pay for training as a truck driver . On the fifth try he passed the written exam. Then he passed the driving test and received his license. He received a job offer in a distant city; caught the bus for that city, arrived and was immediately given a route — Salt Lake, San Francisco, Portland, Boise, then back to Salt Lake. Employment was contingent on a routine physical.

After giving a blood sample my son waited for the physical examination. Through the door came the physician saying: "You are going to the emergency room! Your blood sugars are off the charts!"

The subsequent diagnosis was diabetes, type 1. He was no longer eligible to drive long-haul trucks. He was put back on a bus and returned home.

In this world the rich get richer and the poor get dumped on. Those were the feelings I had upon hearing the news of my son's diabetes, though I used a stronger word than "dumped".

Walked around talking to myself that way for about a month, I did. Only gradually did I become aware of the word "courage". His life made me wonder about mine. Could I face a lifetime of defeat and set-back with the same courage my son did? I don't think so.

His story made me appreciate the level of courage it takes to get out of bed each day to greet 45 years of disappointment and disapproval, all for $5.50 an hour. I came to know I had a son whose courage had been tested to a depth I'd never achieve. And he passed.

So you see why I picked up <u>Nickel and Dimed</u>, Barbara Ehrenreich's book telling of her year trying to get by while working for minimum wage, first in Florida, then in Maine, and finally in Minnesota. Ehrenreich helped me understand how you and I work from a deck stacked in our favor. The poor, you see, must compete with us for housing. That is, they must live reasonably close to us because that is where the service sector jobs are. But Ehrenreich found you couldn't compete in the rental market (save enough for first and last month's rent plus security deposit) unless you had an unusually reliable car, extraordinarily good health, and 70 hours a week on two jobs. But the middle class receives a housing subsidy from the government. It's called the mortgage interest deduction on your tax form. For Ehrenreich that government subsidy amounted to $20,000 a year.

Would you have the courage to play the game, a game where the deck is stacked against you? And how long would you be a player?

Blackberry Theology

Behemoth

Material: Basalt, 45" height, 30" width, 33" depth

Owner: Artist

Blackberry Theology

Took my little self up in the hills south of our place to pick a mess of wild blackberries. It happened because halfway through our wondrous town fireworks down there at Pioneer Park, I suddenly realized, hot damn, Fourth of July, the wild blackberries must be ripe. Rolled out of bed about 5:30 in the a.m. the next day and pulled on heavy work pants and long sleeve shirt to give me a little protection from the barbs, needles, and such. Jumped into my cork boots; then took off for the nearest three-year-old clear-cut.

Three-year-old clear-cuts, don't-cha know, are where you'll find wild things, namely blackberries and black-tailed deer. The deer are after the browse springing up everywhere with tender nutrient-rich leaves and needles. Them wild blackberries are snaking through the grass, over stumps, and up young fir trees on their beautiful pale blue vines looking for both hot sunshine and cool seeps of moisture. All her life, Aunt Illah, my last living Auntie, beat her brother Cletus to the three-year-old clear-cuts, 'cause she'd be out on that hot side hill wallowing around in the undergrowth looking for berries in July, while Uncle Cletus wouldn't get there until October, pussyfooting across the same ground hunting bucks.

Actually, by the time I got up to this particular side hill 't' other day, Illah and Cletus were already there, as were Yvonne and Joy, my deceased sisters. Three other Aunties, Ruby, Dorothy, and Annabelle, plus my parents Rufus and Geraldine, accompanied by Grandma Rosy, were there too. My mother, a little too stout to be jumping stumps, had just found a shady spot when in came William Ridge and Tennessee Tucker, my great grandparents. Wild blackberries, you see, are soul food in our family. Whenever you find a blackberry patch and one of Bill's kin, then the spirit of Bill's family will also be present.

Like I said, I'd gotten out to the patch mighty early and soon found I could pick in only one direction — away from the sun. Ol' Sol was so low on the horizon and so bright I couldn't see a thing when I faced it. I could only stand there fully illuminated in the morning light . After awhile I caught on. "Hey, this is a metaphor for my life," I thought. You see, for thirty years I had turned away from the light. As a little shaver in Eureka in the 30's, I'd gone to the Lutheran Church. Then the P.L.'s timber operations shifted to Yaeger Creek and we moved to Fortuna. As a ten-year-old, I became a Methodist. As a teenager my pals and I ushered every Sunday, went to Methodist Youth Fellowship every Sunday evening, bible school and MYF camp every summer. Eventually, I went off to college in the Bay Area, and by my sophomore year I'd drifted away from the church.

Thirty ears later I got the call to return. The messenger was Everett Moses, an 84-year-old gypo logger from Sweet Home. Old Moses used to pick nuts out at my place every fall to earn a little cash money. Worked in the rain, ate cold beans out of a can, and slept over in the back of his pickup truck. It was a tough buck he earned, you betcha.

At the time, I was divorced and was thrashing around like anyone who has had a twenty-seven-year-old marriage break up. I mean, as a single man, I was living neither the straight nor the narrow, if you get my drift. Heard a knock on the door, opened it, and there, standing in a hard rain and a high wind, was Everett Moses and his sixty-whatever girlfriend. Moses, he shook off the rain water on my kitchen floor, then announced he'd come to sing me a song. No introductions, no howdies, no chit-chat, no nothing. Just pulled up a chair, sat his-self down and took a saw and a fiddle bow out of a case. Proceeded to saw on the saw with his fiddle bow, then opened his mouth and out came three versus of "Amazing Grace".

When he finished his song Moses put his saw and bow back in the case, then banged out the door, girlfriend in tow, calling over his shoulder, "See ya next year."

Within the year, Maude and I married, and months after that we found a church home. You see, even when you turn away from the light for thirty years, it continues to shine on the back of your skull. The universe is always seeking you, inviting you to turn toward the light.

Greetings

My pal Welcome Owsley tries to pass for normal, but most of the time he screws it up royally. Take your plain, ordinary, everyday greeting, "How are you?" What you'd expect to hear from Owsley is a pleasantly vague "fine", wouldn't you? Well, you won't get something normal and expected from that Owsley. Take the other day up on Main Street for example.

I'd been reading most of the morning, but after lunch I'd driven into town and parked up on Main. Owsley, he busts out of the saloon and starts ambling along the sidewalk toward Carlson's Hardware in that lanky, ain't-goin'-nowhere, ain't-got-nothin'-to-do style of his when I spot him and call out, "Hey Welcome, how ya doin'?"

"Bill," sez he, "if I wuz doin' any better they'd put me in jail... I'd be illegal!"

See what I mean? Nobody really expects a serious answer to the question, "How are you?" It just isn't normal. Oh sure, once in a while, someone will answer with, "Okay, and you?", which we all know really means, "Shut up! I don't want to talk about it!" What is normal is a sort of *don't ask, don't tell* agreement. That way, we can all be *safe* hiding in our little closets while sliding to our graves, not knowing anybody really well and not being known by others really well. It's what we call *normal.*

I'd been reading all that morning about a guy, John Wesley, who was definitely not normal. Wesley went around London in the 1750s or so, greeting people with the question, "How goes your soul?" He expected a serious answer.

I'm a Methodist, you see, and John Wesley is the founder of the Methodist movement. I'm in the uncomfortable position of realizing that if I'd gone to Oxford with John Wesley, I wouldn't have had anything to do with him. Nothing. As far as I'm concerned, he was a prissy little wimp obsessed with being holy. He was endlessly creating and revising long lists of holy behaviors, which included fasting certain days every week, daily Biblical studies, and creating and joining various theological discussion groups. These were years of seeking and doubting for Wesley — earnestly seeking God, but filed with doubts that God's grace would find him.

On the voyage back from America to England, Wesley admired the courage and sureness of faith among the Moravians when they encountered fierce storms on the Atlantic. His long, learned discourse on theology were listened to by the Moravians, but then ended with the query, "But you, you John, do you know God?"

Back in London, Wesley resumed his practice of leading religious study groups and participating in still others. He, along with friends, began a regular ministry in prisons, meeting with the condemned and accompanying them in the wagon carrying them through the streets of London to the gallows. At an evening meeting with a group at Aldersgate, Wesley felt his heart strangely warmed. That physical feeling of God's presence set in motion a life-long transforming journey having three themes: God's grace is there for all; in matters of belief, think and let think; there is no holiness save for social holiness.

So I was bending Welcome Owsley's ear with all this reading when Owsley, he stops me with: "My kin were probably in that very jail there in London. I'm Welsh, you know, and them Brits loved nothing better than to be putting my kind behind bars. Why, if that Wesley guy had showed up in our cell asking about our souls, why, we would have told him flat out if our souls were doing any better, they'd put me ...."

Ol' Owsley gets a look on his face, stops; then makes a bee line straight for Randy's to get a strong cup of Joe.

Dopus Opus

Gonna take some risks here folks and throw the theological dice one more time. I may end up looking like a dope. You decide, dear reader, because the topic today is prayer. Who knows, you may decide Oregon Bill is not only dopey but a hypocrite to boot, because, you see, my prayer life is hovering near zero as you read this.

But being regarded as a dope ain't anything new. My daughters, Kristina and Kay, used to regularly call me a "dopus opus". When I asked them what they meant they replied, "Oh, Dad, you are a classic dope! A regular dopus opus!"

As a dopus opus I divvy prayers into two piles — the *speaking* pile and the *listening* pile. Think about it now, most of the time when you pray you have a little one-sided conversation with the infinite. You string words together, silently or out loud, instructing the great power to run the universe thus an' so: dispense a little grace here, a little succor there, and please intercede on behalf of an illness, a poverty, a heartache, a human failing. I pile all these together as *speaking prayers.* However, I think of meditation as making a *listening prayer.*

Joseph Goldstein claims that sorting out meditation systems is simply a matter of mathematics: all meditation systems, either aim for One or Zero — union with God or emptiness. The path to the One is through concentration on Him; the path to the Zero is insight into the voidness of one's mind. Today we'll focus on union, not emptiness.

Been meditating off and on for twenty years or so. When I'm on, I meditate daily for 30 minutes or so. Right now I'm off. Been off ever since our president authorized the use of bombs and bullets against Iraq for what he said were lofty reasons as well as prudently preventive ones. In this endeavor he has said he is strengthened by our prayers.

But the politics of prayer is not the subject under discussion here. What is under discussion is the proposal that we can think of meditation as one form of prayer, a listening prayer.

The first thing we have to do here is to get rid of the idea that meditation is exclusively an Eastern or Buddhist practice. Turns out the very earliest Christian Monks were rigorous and ardent meditators. The earliest Desert Fathers sought out the isolation of the harshest desert to commune with God free of worldly distractions. The rules of living and the meditation practices of these early Christian Monks sought to *still the mind* and thus to draw closer to Him, Christ Jesus.

A fifth century teacher, Hesychius of Jerusalem, describes meditation as a spiritual art that releases one completely from passionate thoughts, words, and evil deeds, and gives a "sure knowledge of God, the Incomprehensible". The Hesychiasts were instructed to still the mind by sitting on a low stool in the solitude of one's cell on first awakening for an hour or so. To collect the mind from its customary wandering and circling and quietly lead it into the heart by way of breathing and repeating this prayer: "Lord Jesus Christ, Son of God, have mercy on me!"

Stilling the mind has been a 20 year problem for me. My form of meditation is to attend to the breath going in and out. But the monkey chatter rattles around my brain cage endlessly. The one time I had a breakthrough occurred about ten years ago when I was meditating late at night. I realized *the me* in me, *my soul*, was hoping to cultivate a quiet mind so that I could become more fully aware of the Christ within. But my brain kept up this ceaseless chatter. Therefore whatever my soul might be, whatever *the me* in me might be, it sure as hell was not the gray matter sitting on top of my spine.

Meditating the next night I became aware that every bit of brain chatter working against stillness of mind, every bit of that chatter, was connected to ego. All of the disruptive, seductive chatter had to do with me looking smart, me being in control, me appearing compassionate, being forgiving, being entertaining, being sexy, cracking wise comments, remembering a friend, and so on. Ego powered every disruptive thought. So, not only was my soul not my brain, it wasn't my ego either. Been contemplating my ego-driven me, is that *me?* ever since.

The feedback on this insight of mine regarding my brain, my ego, and my soul, has been slim and none. But one of them occurred over coffee a few years ago. I wandered in out of the rain one day and sat myself down with a hot steaming latte. Whereupon cousin Kenneth began razzing me about my choice of a highfalutin latte over a plain, ordinary cup of Joe. Somebody objected to cousin's zingers and he announced, "Oh you know Bill, you can't hardly insult him nohow!" And, I thought, "Hot damn, that meditation work pays off!" Even a dopus opus can draw just a little closer to the Christ within.

Nuts Unlimited

For several years now I've crawled around under the trees at our place every fall picking up walnuts and hazelnuts. Washed them nuts, I did, dried them by a wood stove, then took them up to Jim Nelson, the world's best neighbor, where he ran them through the cracker for me. I'd sell them nuts on the cheap, mainly to church friends, to support the various needs of our congregation. Lately, however, our church steeple, the one that blew clean off in the Columbus Day storm of '62, began leaking so bad something had to be done. The few contractors who would even consider the job (it's 80 feet high) offered numbers from $10 to $25 thousand to do the work.

So it was that I told our congregation that this year we were going to take those nutmeats out of the shell and put them into cellophane to raise a wad of money to repair the steeple. They were all invited to a "Nuts for Jesus" work party.

Well now, everybody looked at one another up and down the pews with the silent question on their lips, "Is Bill off-his-meds or what?" But wouldn't you know, that very week "Tell and Sell" had a blurb on the high Omega 3 value of nuts. That blurb wrote our sales slogan for us — *Nuts for Jesus, our Alpha and Our Omega III's!*

Sales so far have passed $1,600 and will probably reach $2,000 before we run out of nuts. The work has given us both a giggle and a surprise. First the surprise.

We make dinner for 50 to 80 low-income people at our Friday night get together called "Manna." Additionally, an AA group meets at our church, as does a drug co-dependency group. One night at one of our nut parties we looked around and counted 25 people in attendance, 12 of who were from those three groups using our church. Warmed our hearts, and theirs, you betcha!

Now for the giggle: Nuts for Jesus signs draw a lot of snickers. Most of that laughter, but not all, is good hearted. As you well know, folks who attend church are pretty widely regarded as judgmental stick-in-the-muds. We church people are not real practiced at light hearted, mirthful worship. The giggle we found in our Nuts for Jesus project was the playfulness of it all.

But learning how to romp and play in God's presence has been an old, old problem for the human critter. Listen to Hafiz, a Sufi mystic, writing a note on this issue way back in the 1300s:

> There is only one rule
> On this Wild Playground.
>
> For every sign Hafiz has ever seen
> Reads the same.
>
> "Have fun, my dear; my dear, have fun,
> In the Beloved's Divine
> Game,
>
> Oh, in the Beloved's
> Wonderful
> Game."

Love the Water More

What we've got here is a thirteenth century poet stirring the pot of Manna up in Sweet Home, Oregon. Check it out. Manna, you know, is the weekly free meal located at the Methodist Church in Sweet Home. Jelaluddin Rummi, the Sufi poet, commented on what we've got going, though his commentary was delivered seven centuries ago. What he was remarking on was the fact that Tim and Bonnie came over from the Fir Lawn Lutheran Church to help out after they heard about the weekly free meal. Tim settled in washing dishes, while Bonnie helped cook and serve. They were soon joined by Clarence and Annona from the Presbyterian church. The two of them took to setting up the dessert table then cleaning the dining room tables after dinner. Right now there are members from four additional churches helping to put the meal together and to swamp out afterwards. We can serve 75 to 80 meals of a Friday so there is plenty of getting ready and cleaning up to do.

It didn't take Tim long before he started sitting in on our Methodist Men's Club. Clarence dropped by too. Before you know it we decided to transform the group calling it the Sweet Home Men's Service Group. The new outfit is for churched men generally in Sweet Home. Additionally, we are looking around for synagogued men, templed men, mosqued and Sangha men, too. We'll try to rope them into the Manna work. If we don't have enough work to keep them hombres off the streets and out of lowlife bars, we plan to distribute honey-do request slips to the elderly, widowed, or single women in town who need a roof patched, a garden spaded, or some other job they haven't gotten around to. There'll be plenty of work to keep all hands busy.

Rummi put it like this: "Love the pitcher less; love the water more." That is, a church (or mosque, synagogue, temple or Sangha) is mainly a community through which one might encounter the sacred. That encounter is the water; love it more. Alas, a slew of people today regard organized religion as a bunch of ceremonies and rituals designed to prevent exactly that — encounters with the sacred. Up in Sweet Home Rummi is leading us to try to change all that.

"Love the pitcher less; love the water more." Jalaluddin Rummi, b. 1207 A.D.

Boundary and Horizon

I've taken three steps on my spiritual path. However, one of those steps involved going to church. And Oregon, you know, is the least churched state in the Union. So Bill is clearly out of step with most Oregonians. Listen up then and you'll see just how peculiar the old gaffer has become in taking those three steps away from boundary and toward horizon.

First you gotta know that I boycotted church for 30 years or so. That boycott happened because life became for me, a throw of the dice. Folks, our existence is all chance and accident devoid of meaning, or so it seemed to me after the death of my father. Dad's work pattern was to fall timber with his partner all morning. After lunch each partner would take his separate chain saw and buck up the fallen trees into merchantable lengths. On the afternoon of my father's death a standing tree that had been knocked by another falling tree in the morning, that tree gave way in the wet winter soil in the afternoon and fell, crushing my father in the duff on a side hill up Yaeger Creek. His partner sawed Dad free and got him down to the speeder where he was lain down causing his crushed lungs to fill with blood drowning him on the way out of the woods.

Like I say, step one involved about 30 years thinking off and on about the pointlessness of our existence within a universe of random events devoid of meaning or purpose. In those years I met and married Maude and we both took up the study of aikido. It's a martial art built around the notion of Chi or Ki, the life force extant in the universe. Aikido asserts that our normal subconscious is filled with anger, conflict, competition and so forth. The image is one of a tea cup filled with muddy water (the subconscious). The spiritual and martial arts task is to experience and learn to extend plus Ki thereby adding pure water drop by drop to slowly change the composition of the muddy water in our little tea cup. The discipline consists of practicing Ki exercises, meditating in a practice called Ki breathing, and finally to learn the throws that neutralize an attacker. You are responsible both for your own safety and for the safety of your attacker.

The dominant analogy of this work is that of the iceberg which shows only a small portion of its mass above the surface of the water. So too the human being relying only on its conscious mind uses but a small portion of the power that is theirs. Developing plus Ki in the subconscious is the path to realizing that greater power. As you learn to extend plus Ki life gets easier, more fun, and more effective.

It took 10 years of study but my experiences with aikido convinced me there is a force called Ki in this universe that is positive, life affirming, and growth promoting. Yes, this life does include inexplicable cruelty, accident, and randomness. But there is also Ki, life energy.

Step two involved a realization about myself. That is, left to my own devices, I tend to be spiritually lazy . I gradually came to know that I'm a person that needs community in order to become a fuller, more complete me. That may not be true for you. Your spiritual work may proceed quite nicely, "thank you," without the necessity of community. But that is not me.

Finally, if community is required of me, what sort of community should I join? Surprisingly, this question was answered while listening to the Dalai Lama. Like a lot of you, Buddhism intrigues me. So Maude and I went to San Francisco to sit on a side hill for two days, while the Dalai Lama spoke. He counseled us not to become estranged from our Western theological heritage — our Judeo-Christian deep history. It is a powerful source. "Do it well," counseled the Dalai Lama.

Thus, I attend church. My faith community celebrates questions rather than answers. Standard church going seems to emphasize boundaries. A boundary system is set, unchanging, and complete. We try to be non-standard by emphasizing horizon rather than boundary. A horizon alters every time you walk toward it. The horizon of our existence is contemplated as we ask and pursue questions.

What a peculiar path. And so un-Oregonian too. But, that's Bill.

A Throw of the Dice

Sometimes you whomp up a goal that is so fundamental you go ahead and throw the dice even though the chances of succeeding are slim and none. We've got a deal like that up in Sweet Home. Here's the story.

Our church up there feeds poor people twice a week. We grow a garden to help supply the meal. And, we peddle nuts to earn dollars to support the whole enterprise. All that is pretty ordinary. Many civic and church groups all across America do similar things.

What is out of the ordinary is that we have set a five year goal to empower the Manna community ("Manna" is the name for the meal we serve) to feed themselves. In five years we intend for the Manna folks themselves to have taken over preparing the meal, to have taken over growing the garden, and to have taken over the business of selling hazelnuts, walnuts, nut candies, and gift boxes. That is our roll of the dice — to empower a community of poor people to serve one another. We could very well fail.

Most especially we could fail because we are so ignorant. But, then, nearly everybody is as dumb as we are. Lots of folks know how to do *for* the poor. Damn few know how to go about doing *with* the poor.

However, we have been working at our ignorance problem for a few years and we have learned a few things. We have learned about time and trust; we have learned about job creation; we have learned about community building.

Most people come sit at the table as separate individuals. Community consciousness has to be nudged into existence. That nudging starts simply enough by taking off your apron and sitting down to join in the meal yourself. That is the way you become acquainted with and maybe even friends with your dinner companions. Because, you see, we got taught early on that we were not serving just physical hungers, but social and spiritual hunger as well. Our "Manna" regulars show up 2 and 3 hours before dinner is served. It is a place and time to ease loneliness by drinking coffee and shooting the breeze. Moreover, breaking bread together is a sacred act. That feeling tone we have come to believe permeates the dining room.

After 4 or 5 years this community consciousness building seems to be taking place. Recently, we added a second meal, a Tuesday gathering to augment the regular meal every Friday. To our solid delight a number of Manna regulars stepped forward to help prep, help serve, to wash dishes, and to clean up. Interestingly too, individuals from three or four other churches in town now regularly volunteer at the Manna meal. A spirit of community seems to be forming.

We have also learned about job creation. Many of our Manna regulars are on Social Security or SSI. They have shown us that after they pay the rent, pay the electric bill, buy meds, and so on, they have only about $20 left of disposable income. In their lives a cold snap, a dead battery, or a flat tire is a major financial challenge. So when you announce a job everyone is all ears. This happened to us after we gathered, washed, dried, and cracked several hundred pounds of walnuts. We started out separating nut meats from nut shells, using church volunteers, but it got too much for us. So now we pay Manna regulars by the ounce to come to the church to separate out nut meat. This led in turn to creating a second set of jobs — selling the product at holiday bazaars, craft fairs, and elsewhere. Job creation is our secret weapon in our struggle against hunger — physical, social, and spiritual.

Building trust, we have been taught, takes time and happens one person at a time. We learn and relearn this lesson every time we are silly enough to think that making a general announcement at dinner will get results. It doesn't. You build trust slowly and you build it across the dinner table talking one on one with someone who regards you as a friend, someone who knows you and knows you are interested in them as an individual.

So, we have thrown the dice — empowering a poor community to serve themselves. We are working at overcoming our ignorance — how do you do it? We've got 4 more years to work at our goal.

We shall see if we succeed or fail.

About the Author

Rod Fielder was found in a goosepen and grew up in a small community in the Pacific Northwest. He went away to college only because his arm wasn't strong enough to play professional baseball. Moreover, he wasn't a long ball hitter.

Professor Fielder taught at San Jose State College, Stanford University, Michigan State University, Claremont Graduate School, and Oregon State University. He was the designer and general editor of the Holt Databank System, an elementary school social studies instructional system. He edited and published two childrens' textbooks, Get Oregonized and Global Oregon.

Presently, Rod farms a hazelnut orchard near Brownsville, Oregon where he and his wife Sara have restored the Hugh Fields House (1855), a Greek Revival Territorial home.

His "Oregon Bill" yarns first appeared as a column in the *Brownsville Times.*